P9-EDA-642

THE GOLDEN HILLS OF CALIFORNIA
VOLUME TWO

Masri, Allan.
The golden hills of
California : illustrated
1979-c1983.
33305220081594
cu   08/28/21

THE GOLDEN HILLS OF CALIFORNIA
VOLUME TWO

A Descriptive Guide to the Mother Lode Counties
of the Northern Mines, including Placer, El Dorado,
Sacramento, Nevada, Yuba, Sierra, and Plumas

With historical photographs, maps, points of interest,
natural phenomena and historical highlights.

By Allan Masri

SANTA CLARA COUNTY LIBRARY

3 3305 22008 1594

WESTERN TANAGER PRESS, SANTA CRUZ

122580

SANTA CLARA COUNTY LIBRARY
SAN JOSE, CALIFORNIA

Copyright © 1983 by Western Tanager Press
All rights reserved. No part of this book may be reproduced
in any form without the written consent of the publisher.

Maps by Linda Knudson
Cover Photo by John Senser
Manufactured in the United States of America/Acid-free paper

Western Tanager Press
1111 Pacific Avenue
Santa Cruz, California 95060

Library of Congress Catalog Number: 78-65266
ISBN: 0-934136-21-1

Contents

Maps

Illustrations

Preface

California has grown at an incredible rate since the second World War. Thousands of new residents know little or nothing about the traditions of the state they live in. Furthermore, many are seeking an escape from the crowded city landscape and the headaches of modern life. Therefore there is a real need for a book such as this at this time, even though it incorporates no startling new discoveries or theoretical breakthroughs.

Naturally, when dealing with the past one must always yield to the advice of others, whether they be scholars or enthusiasts. I have had the good fortune to find assistance at the Bancroft Library and at the western library of the University of the Pacific; the Chambers of Commerce for Auburn, Grass Valley, and Placerville; the museums at the North Star Power House, Downieville, and at the state parks, namely the Gold Discovery Park at Coloma, the Empire Mine Park in Grass Valley, Old Town Sacramento, Malakoff Diggins, and Plumas-Eureka; in addition, I have had the personal support and guidance of John Caswell and J. A. Smurr; and finally, the aid of Miss Holly Holst. The typing of the manuscript is my own work, however, and so is the responsibility for all the errors which may be found within these pages.

Any description of the golden hills must begin in the far distant past, before the dawn of history, with the birth of the mountains. In that time beyond recall, the mighty peaks of the Sierra Nevada range were lifted to their present lofty height by some force of nature about which we can only theorize. The foothills to the west are older than the mountains themselves, but they assumed their present aspect at the same time.

The mountains and the hills which lead us up to the ridges like a flight of stairs are remarkable first for their beauty. Desolate reaches of the high country seem as remote from the world of our everyday cares as the mountains on the moon. The hills, too, appear barren and lifeless much of the year, for they are covered by a sparse layer of clump grass of the kind that led Mark Twain to remark that everything in California looks better from a distance: The grassy meadows of springtime may beckon the weary wayfarer but they will not permit him to rest upon them, for the grass is stiff and grows in clumps surrounded by patches of bare earth.

The celebrated author of *Tom Sawyer* did admit the beauty, however, and the modern visitor will be struck immediately by the primeval quality of the landscape: Wildflowers spread their varicolored petals in the shade of dappled oaks and gnarled "digger" pines; the forests above spring right out of rocks covered by lichens in fanciful shapes and colors that give the impression they were spattered on the ground by some gigantic disciple of Jackson Pollack.

Though the grizzly bear that graces the California state flag was long ago hunted to extinction by hungry settlers and nervous cattlemen, many of the original inhabitants of this land still persist in their natural environment. Some, like the colorful warblers and sleek grey squirrels, advertise their presence to every visitor. Others are more shy: The lonely coyote hunts at dusk in brush that matches the color of his coat precisely; the skunk and possum come out only at night, seldom to be seen save when caught in the glare of an automobile's headlights as they scurry across the highway; and the graceful deer often gaze at motorists but keep so still that their presence may be overlooked by the unwary.

Other, more sinister creatures are seldom seen. The tarantula hides in his hole during the daytime, save in the fall, when these hairy spiders may sometimes be seen crawling across roadways. The rattlesnake is also shy of human contact, though he seems attracted to members of his own kind, for sometimes nests containing great numbers of these deadly reptiles are found by startled visitors to remote places.

The streams serve as protective cover for many species of trout and bass worthy of any fisherman's interest, while the rocks in the creekbeds conceal tiny crayfish esteemed by many as delicacies and easily plucked from their hiding places by a skilled hand.

To the blessings of nature, the hills add the fascination of history. Buildings of hand-hewn stone stand as mute witnesses to the pageant of the Gold Rush. Neglected graveyards mark the sites of once-prosperous communities now vanished without a trace. If the stones could speak, they would undoubtedly tell more fascinating tales than any to which I can aspire. Nevertheless, I submit this small volume for your perusal in the hope that you may find something of interest here—and with the assurance that you will find your explorations of the golden hills more exciting when you know more of their history.

THE GOLDEN HILLS OF CALIFORNIA
VOLUME TWO

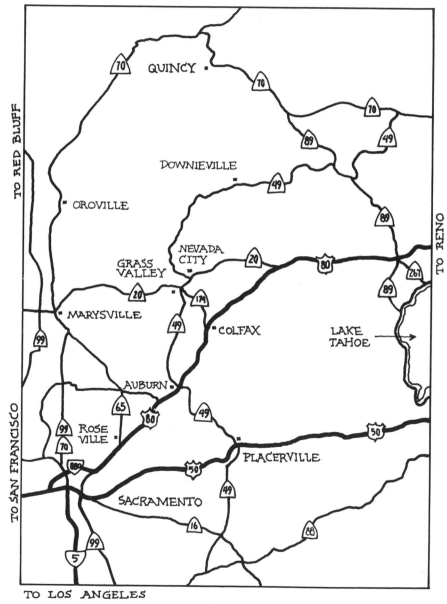

MAP 1.

Part One:

The Cradle of Gold

Highway 50 leads directly into the heart of the gold country along much the same route that the first gold-seekers took in their headlong rush for real or imagined riches. The country through which it passes bears the name of a fabulous country where gold was so plentiful that it took the place of make-up. The following story was told to the Spanish Conquistadores by the natives of Central and South America:

Somewhere (no one could ever be very precise about the location), there is a land where gold dust is as abundant as the game in the forest or the fruit on the trees. The king of this land is so wealthy that he causes himself to be painted with gold every morning, and his skin shines like the sun. Every night this covering must be washed off so as not to disturb the sleep of the monarch, and every morning an entirely new coat must be applied. The king is known as the gilded one— El Dorado.

The Spaniards believed this tale and set off in search of the fabulous kingdom. It is one of the odd quirks of history that they never found the gold of California, for if any place could rightly claim to be the land of El Dorado, this was it. For thousands of years, gold sands, washed down by winter freshets from deposits in the mountains, had settled into the crevices of the streams. But the natives, separated from the rest of the world by the chain of mountains that still impedes

traffic to the east, never learned the value of gold. Instead
they bartered with strings of seashells obtained at ruinous
prices from their neighbors who dwelt by the sea. All around
them lay fabulous wealth, but they never saw it, and neither
did the Spaniards.

Folsom

The downtown area of Folsom still preserves the memory
of its frontier past in its old buildings and rustic atmosphere.
After the discovery of gold on the American River in 1848,
Folsom quickly became a trade depot astride the major route
from Sacramento to the goldfields. Other roads led from
Folsom to Auburn and the mining regions to the south. The
first rail line in California, the Sacramento Valley Railroad,
reached Folsom in 1856, and the small town was transformed
overnight into a major trading center.

Theodore N. Judah

This line was largely the creation of a young engineer
named Theodore N. Judah, a little-renowned dreamer who
never lived to see how his crackpot ideas made millions for
his one-time partners. Born in 1826 at Bridgeport, Connec-
ticut, Judah learned the trade of engineering on the Erie
Canal, that marvelous school for American builders. His
imagination was fired by the discovery of gold on the Pacific
slope, though in this respect he differed not a bit from
thousands of fellow Easterners. He was not interested in
gold itself, however, but in a railroad to be constructed on a
scale never before dreamed of, a railroad that would connect
the new state of California with the rest of the United States.
His ambitions quickly earned him the nickname "crazy
Judah."

Young Judah traveled to the west coast in pursuit of his
dream in the early 1850s. Here he worked for several different railroad companies, including the Sacramento Valley
line. He himself was among the first to ride the rails he had
helped construct—in a handcar over a distance of 400 feet.
But the Sacramento Valley Railroad soon bogged down, and
Judah organized his own company, the Central Pacific
Railroad.

To raise the necessary funds for his project, Judah enlisted

Gold in California

It is difficult to understand why gold remained so long undiscovered in California, considering that so much of it was on the surface, even in those parts of the country already inhabited by whites. The Indians, who will search assiduously for the flints they require for arrow-heads, do not seem to have been aware of the existence of gold on the plains, although the savages of the as yet unexplored mountain districts are found with gold in their possession. The early Spanish priests evidently sought for it without success, judging from the old shafts that have been sunk on part of the banks of the Stanislaus River; and yet these explorations were ineffectually made in the centre of a rich district, and by a class of gentlemen who were never in the habit of overlooking a good thing. Some of the best diggings have been discovered by market-gardeners, who have chosen some apparently valueless tract for the purpose of cabbage growing, and it is a fact that one man with more energy than agricultural experience, who was abusing the earth for producing cabbages that were all stalk, found on rooting up one very lengthy specimen, that a piece of gold adhered to the roots.

It is possible that both my readers have heard of a certain pig that could only be induced to go in one direction by being at the onset driven in another; it is somewhat this way with the search for gold. Start on a voyage of discovery for copper or coal, and you will probably, if in a gold region, tumble down and break your nose over a nugget as large as a paving-stone; but if you give chase to the seductive metal itself, the toil of a lifetime will very likely not counterbalance the first week's privation.

Frank Marryat, *Mountains and Molehills*, 1855

the aid of the merchants of Sacramento, all of whom stood to profit by his venture. Four of them are worthy of mention here: Mark Hopkins and Collis P. Huntington, who were partners in a hardware store; Leland Stanford, a wholesale grocer; and Charles Crocker, a dry-goods merchant. All men of modest means, these small businessmen would soon become the most powerful men in California, known to all as the Big Four.

The Big Four

One might suppose that Judah, who organized the company and surveyed the most feasible route through the mountains, might also have gained fame and fortune, but it was not to be. Judah soon quarreled with his partners over their methods of conducting the business, for they contracted all work on the railroad to companies which they themselves owned. The last straw came when the other four partners wanted to move the Sierra Nevada mountains twelve miles west. As long as the railroad was being built in the Sacramento Valley, the company could only receive $16,000 per mile in low-interest loans from the federal government; once the mountains were reached, however, the amount would be increased to $48,000. The Big Four managed to convince the government that the Sierra began twelve miles farther to the west than they really did and thereby netted a windfall profit of over $400,000.

Judah hurried east to persuade Wall Street bankers to buy out his partners and enable him to assume complete control of the company. But in the days before the railroad the shortest route to New York lay across the Isthmus of Panama, and it was there that Judah contracted yellow fever. He died shortly after he reached New York City. The Big Four, who subsequently named many of the towns along the route of the railroad after many lesser men, never named as much as a whistle stop after the genius who planned the whole operation. His name is, however, memorialized for thousands of commuters on San Francisco's N-Judah streetcar line.

Folsom is situated beside a lake formed by waters backed up behind Folsom Dam. This lake covers several sites of importance to the early history of the region. The ones with the most interesting stories are Mormon Island, Negro Hill, and Mountaineer House.

Mormon Island

Mormon Island was a large island in the American River.

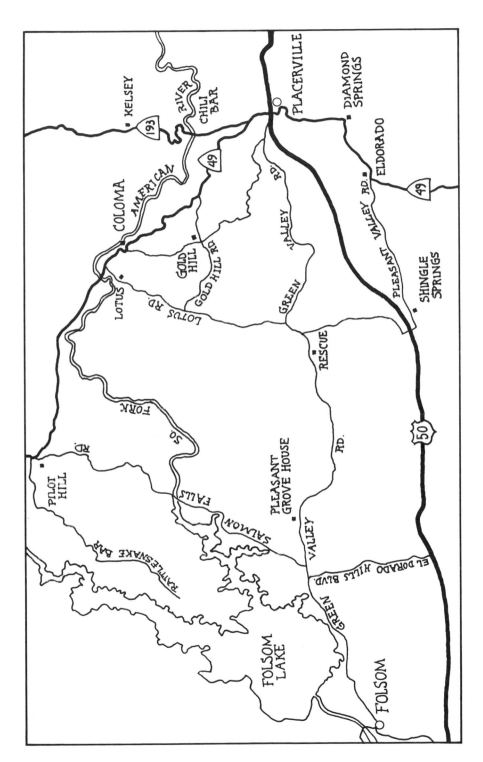

MAP 2.

Gold: The First Reports

Monday, May 29. Our town was startled out of its quiet dreams to-day, by the announcement that gold had been discovered on the American Fork. The men wondered and talked, and the women too; but neither believed. The sibyls were less skeptical; they said the moon had, for several nights, appeared not more than a cable's length from the earth; that a white raven had been seen playing with an infant; and that an owl had rung the church bells.

Monday, June 5. Another report reached us this morning from the American Fork. The rumor ran, that several workmen, while excavating for a mill-race, had thrown up little shining scales of a yellow ore, that proved to be gold; that an old Sonorian, who had spent his life in gold mines, pronounced it the genuine thing. Still the public incredulity remained, save here and there a glimmer of faith, like the flash of a fire-fly at night. One good old lady, however, declared that she had been dreaming of gold every night for several weeks, and that it had so frustrated her simple household economy, that she had relieved her conscience, by confessing to her priest—

"Absolve me, father, of that sinful dream."

Walter Colton, *Three Years in California*, 1850

Sam Brannan

Settled by the Mormons who were employed at Sutter's Mill at the time of the discovery, Mormon Island was one of the very first camps dedicated to the pursuit of the elusive yellow metal. The leader of these Mormons was Sam Brannan, a shrewd businessman who intended to capitalize on his heaven-sent opportunity for riches. Brannan invested heavily in San Francisco real estate and various transport enterprises, including steamboats to ply the Sacramento River. The source of his great wealth was not hard to find: he collected a tithe of one-third of the gold produced by Mormons on Mormon Island.

That Brannan's operations had not the approval of Brigham Young is clear: Young ordered all Mormons out of California and back to Utah so that they would not become tainted by civilization (if the mass of boisterous mankind that was the gold rush deserves that name), but a few chose to remain and hunt their fortunes with Brannan.

Sam Brannan's greatest claim to fame was the part he played in making public the discovery of gold on the American River. Sutter and Marshall were trying to keep their find a secret, but Brannan wanted more miners to come and start buying provisions at his store. So one day he filled a jar with gold dust and rode down the main street of San Francisco, shouting, "Gold from the American River!" The residents got the message. Within a few days of his arrival hardly a man capable of lifting a pick was left in the city. All had departed for the goldfields—though Brannan stayed behind to buy up city lots for pennies on the dollar.

Brannan may have been a scoundrel in some ways, but he was also a just man. When the vigilante group known as the Hounds attacked Chileans in San Francisco, Brannan led the crowd that put the Hounds to flight. Greedy he may have been, but he shared the same fate as so many other would-be tycoons in the early days: wiped out by one of the frequent panics, he spent his declining years in poverty.

Near Mormon Island was a camp that bore the name Negro Hill, since it was settled mainly by black miners. Soon driven off their claims by unscrupulous whites, the blacks began working another placer nearby.

Negro Hill

The Mountaineer House was a typical example of a wayside inn. These inns sprang up everywhere along the main thoroughfares between the mining camps during the 1850s, but Mountaineer House had an additional claim to fame as the headquarters for members of the notorious gang of outlaws led by Tom Bell. Born Thomas Hodges, a native of Tennessee, Bell drifted to California with the intention of practicing medicine there. Doctors were by no means a scarce commodity in the goldfields, however, so Bell soon drifted into other pursuits, first as a miner, then as a gambler, and finally as a highwayman. Around 1854 he began to

Mountaineer House

Tom Bell

PORTAIT OF Mᴿ MARSHAL, TAKEN FROM NATURE AT THE TIME WHEN HE MADE THE DISCOVERY OF GOLD IN CALIFORNIA

Portrait of Marshall (*Courtesy, The Bancroft Library*)

organize a gang of desperadoes who would terrorize the whole length of the goldfields. As many as fifty men were members of the gang, known to each other ony by a set of prearranged signals and the device of a bullet tied to the end of a string. This anonymity made the gang difficult to break up, for a single member had very little information to impart to the authorities.

Tom Bell, tall, handsome despite a broken nose, and wily as a coyote, led his gang of cutthroats for two years before finishing his career at the end of a rope. After an unsuccessful raid on the Marysville-Comptonville stage that would have netted $100,000 in gold, Bell was apprehended by pursuing deputies in 1856.

Pleasant Grove House

If you drive along Green Valley Road (which runs from Folsom to Placerville, parallel to Highway 50) you will be following approximately the same route as the daring riders of the Pony Express during 1860 and 1861. Pleasant Grove House, about nine and a half miles east of Folsom, on the left after the El Dorado Hills turnoff, was one of the 75 relay stations where the teenage riders changed horses and galloped away on fresh mounts without stopping to catch their breath.

Pony Express

Although the Pony Express captured the imagination of Americans for all time, few today know much about it. It was started by a stage line essentially as a publicity stunt to demonstrate the superiority of a central overland stage route over the southern route followed by the Butterfield stages.

Before it had been in operation a whole year, the Civil War had started and the southern route had to be abandoned. The Express constituted an enormous drain on the resources of its operators, but still they persisted on an eleven-day schedule until the Pacific telegraph line was completed on October 26, 1861.

One mile beyond the Pleasant Grove House is the Green Valley House, an example of the early Californian roadside hotels that form such an important part of the frontier lore. Here it was that miners on their way to the diggins passed the night and listened as old-timers weaved yarns about lakes whose shores were lined with gold nuggets; here, highwaymen sat and drank whisky while waiting for the signal that the express stage was on its way; here, successful miners, their pockets lined with gold dust, flirted with barmaids on the way back to their sweethearts and home, or engaged in a friendly game of chance that often as not sent them back to the mines.

Green Valley House

Most early hotels stood at important crossroads, where towns later grew up around them. The Green Valley House was built where the early road forked: Coloma lay to the north, to the east was Hangtown. When enough houses had been built at this point to justify calling it a town, the name of Rescue was applied. Early records do not explain whether some dramatic event in the neighborhood occasioned the name, or whether it was merely the provisions that were sold here that rescued many a weary traveler from hunger and fatigue.

Rescue

It is not hard to imagine the difficulites encountered by the miners on their way to the diggins in the early days. As you look around you, remember that there were no roads, only narrow wagon tracks. The sun was every bit as hot in summer as it is today, while winter rains turned thick, dusty trails into veritable quagmires. Whatever a miner wanted, he had to carry with him; unless, of course, he could afford to pay the freighting costs of $30 per 100 pounds between Sacramento and Coloma. Once he reached the mines, ordinary articles of clothing, blankets, food, and the like could be bought only at exorbitant prices. Tin pans—the first necessity for a miner—went for $16 apiece. Fresh apples cost a dollar-fifty each, but might have been worth the price, since scurvy was a major complaint among the miners. Small wonder that those who struck it rich in the mines were more often than not merchants rather than miners.

Coloma—Gold Discovery Site State Historical Park

Before the white men came to claim its riches, Coloma (north from Placerville on Highway 49) was the home of a band of Maidu Indians. These people were peaceful and gentle, unlike the Plains tribes the miners were familiar with. The newcomers hated and feared them all the same, for most pioneers had had run-ins with Comanche or Pawnee and many could count friends or relatives slain in Indian raids. The town takes its name from the tribe that was living here when James Marshall first arrived on the scene looking for a suitable location for a sawmill. Marshall and his boss, John Augustus Sutter, used Indians as workhands whenever possible, for the simple reason that no one else was available. Only a few Americans had penetrated this far west in 1848, but apparently some of them had settled near the river, for its name was given by John C. Frémont in 1844 as *Rio de los Americanos*—American River.

John Sutter

Sutter himself was not an American. Like so many of the men who came to California in the early days, Sutter was an impractical dreamer. Sutter's dream was to found a new Switzerland in this remote corner of the world. In 1840, after years of waiting, Sutter received permission from the Mexican governor, Juan Bautista Alvarado, to settle in the Sacramento Valley. He named his rancho "New Helvetia" and employed Hawaiians and Americans as well as Californians. In 1841 he furthered his plans to build a feudal state in the New World when he obtained forty cannon from the Russians at Fort Ross and then built a fortress to hold them.

Sutter threw open his gates to American immigrants of every description. His strategic location and fortifications made him stronger than the Mexican authorities, who would have sought to exclude the Americans. One such American was James Marshall.

James Marshall

Marshall was a simple man. Born in New Jersey in 1810, he heeded the westward call that infected the entire nation

Marshall Discovers Gold

One morning in January [January 24, 1848], it was a clear, cold morning; I shall never forget that morning. As I was taking my usual walk along the race, after shutting off the water, my eye was caught by a glimpse of something shining in the bottom of the ditch. There was about a foot of water running there. I reached my hand down and picked it up; it made my heart thump for I felt certain it was gold. The piece was about half the size and of the shape of a pea. Then I saw another piece in the water. After taking it out, I sat down and began to think right hard. I thought it was gold, and yet it did not seem to be of the right color; all the gold coin I had seen was of a reddish tinge; this looked more like brass.

I recalled to mind all the metals I had ever seen or heard of, but I could find none that resembled this. Suddenly the idea flashed across my mind that it might be iron pyrites. I trembled to think of it! This question could soon be determined. Putting one of the pieces on hard river stone, I took another and commenced hammering it. It was soft and didn't break; it therefore must be gold, but largely mixed with some other metal, very likely silver; for pure gold, I thought, would certainly have a brighter color.

When I returned to our cabin for breakfast, I showed the two pieces to my men. They were all a good deal excited, and had they not thought that the gold only existed in small quantities they would have abandoned everything and left me to finish the job alone. However, to satisfy them, I told them that as soon as we had the mill finished we would devote a week or two to gold hunting and see what we could make out of it.

James Marshall, *Century Magazine*, 1891

in those days, moving to Missouri and then to California, where he arrived in 1845. Sutter found work for him as he had for many others. In 1847 they decided to build a sawmill and float logs down the American River to help build New Helvetia. The scheme was a wild one: no one has ever succeeded in floating logs down the streams of the Sierra, whose precipitous courses are strewn with boulders and other obstructions. But Marshall was ready to try. He had worked as a carpenter and farmer in Missouri, but what was more important, he knew how a sawmill should look and function. He knew how to build a channel, called a millrace, with gates at either end to permit the rushing waters of the river flow into the channel and turn the saw.

Together with twelve Mormons, including a woman and her two children, and with the assistance of the friendly natives, Marshall completed work on Sutter's mill by the beginning of 1848. On January 24, while making a routine inspection of the millrace for signs of erosion, Marshall noticed a few yellow flakes of metal among the sand which had accumulated at the bottom of the channel. Could this be gold? he wondered.

The existence of gold had long been suspected in California. A mine was actually in operation in Los Angeles County, but its output was not very encouraging. There had been many rumored discoveries of precious metals, but none proved substantial. So it was left to Marshall to make the first important discovery that would lead to the greatest gold rush in the history of the world.

Marshall's first thought was to verify his discovery and tell his employer about it. Accordingly, he took a few large specimens and rode to Sutter's Fort. There, with the aid of an encyclopedia, the crucial tests were made. It was indeed gold. Sutter was afraid the discovery would lead his laborers to desert the mill and farm to seek fortune on their own, and he wanted to keep the discovery secret. But already upon his return Marshall found his mill workers spending their time prying gold nuggets out of crevices with pen-knives. Before long nearly every able-bodied man in the region was working in the goldfields, and more were on their way from every corner of the globe.

The gold rush made many men wealthy, but it ruined

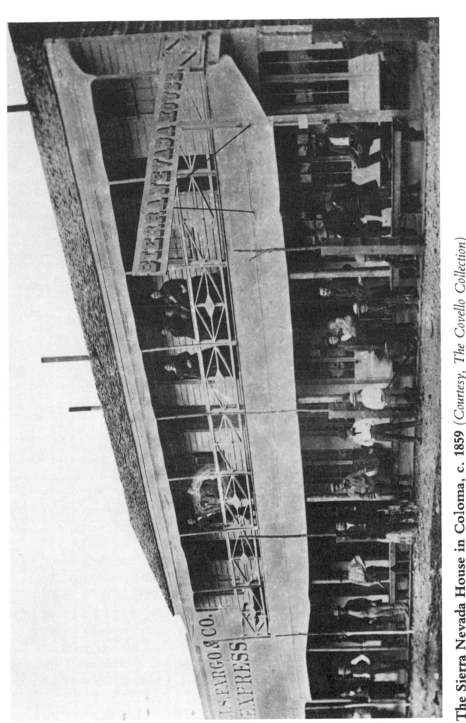

The Sierra Nevada House in Coloma, c. 1859 (*Courtesy, The Covello Collection*)

Sutter. The land around his mill was soon overrun by prospectors and the mill itself destroyed. Still, Sutter would have been able to prosper, as Brannan did, by establishing a store and selling provisions to the miners, and in fact tried just that. Sutter's agents, however, proved to be rogues who robbed him when his back was turned. Sutter, so generous to so many parties of immigrants, did not have a head for business. Disheartened by his failures, he neglected his farms and went to San Francisco on a mad spree.

When Sutter's grown son arrived from Switzerland, it seemed for a while that he would set his father's affairs in order, but the elder Sutter left on another spree and his fortunes collapsed irreparably. Sutter blamed the government of the United States for his misfortunes, and instituted a series of law suits to recover a portion of what was due him. In a sense he was right, for the government had refused to recognize his property rights during the first years of the rush, when millions in gold were removed from the area around Coloma. The government felt this would encourage immigration to the newly acquired territory.

At any rate, Sutter left his vast holdings in 1869—he was then sixty-six years old—and went to Washington, D.C., to press his claims in person. He spent eleven fruitless years entangled in the federal bureaucracy before he died, almost penniless, in 1880.

Marshall's fate was a little better, largely because he did not have so much to lose. Nevertheless, what little he had was soon gone. He tried to make a go of it as a miner but failed, as did the vast majority of his fellow miners. Having panned out at one location, he moved on, hoping to discover gold elsewhere. Indeed, he believed he had a secret ability to find precious metals and was foolish enough to boast of his powers to other prospectors. From then on, Marshall got no rest: prospectors followed him everywhere he went, begging him to tell them where they would find gold and then threatening him with violence when he could not.

Marshall's later years were filled with bitterness and a struggle for existence. He engaged in various activities, as befitted his character. He ran a blacksmith shop, planted grapevines, and helped develop mines around Kentucky Flat. He even went on lecture tours and sold autographed pictures

Sutter's Side of the Story

So soon as the secret was out my laborers began to leave me, in small parties first, but then all left, from the clerk to the cook, and I was in great distress; only a few mechanics remained to finish some very necessary work which they had commenced, and about eight invalids, who continued slowly to work a few teams, to scrape out the mill race at Brighton. The Mormons did not like to leave my mill unfinished, but they got the gold fever like everybody else.

. . . What a great misfortune was this sudden gold discovery for me! It has just broken up and ruined my hard, restless, and industrious labors, connected with many dangers of life, as I had many narrow escapes before I became properly established. From my mill buildings I reaped no benefit whatever, the mill stones even have been stolen and sold.

. . . By this sudden discovery of the gold, all my great plans were destroyed. Had I succeeded with my mills and manufactories for a few years before the gold was discovered, I should have been the richest citizen on the Pacific shore . . .

John A. Sutter, *Hutchings' California Magazine*, 1857

of himself. In his later years, he tried to force the state government to give him a pension in honor of his great service to the state's development, but without success. He died in Kelsey in 1885 and was buried on a hill overlooking the site of his momentous discovery.

The recognition denied James Marshall during his lifetime has been accorded him after his death, for the park at Coloma celebrates his memory. Here you will find a large statue whose outstretched finger points to the discovery site. The museum holds many memorabilia which he collected in his blacksmith shop. His sawmill has been reconstructed by

the state and is one of the most popular tourist spots in the
gold country—not a bad memorial for a man whose only
claim to fame was a stroll along a river that could have been
made by any other man alive—in fact, one of the Mormons
later claimed that her young son had made the discovery
first!

The museum at Coloma is well worth a visit. Besides the
Marshall exhibits, it contains a Concord stage and many
Maidu   Maidu artifacts. The Concord stage was the vehicle that
plied the stage routes in the days before the railroad. Its most
notable feature is the thoroughbraces, a system of suspension
that kept the passengers from being shaken to death when
the wooden wheels rolled across rocky roadbeds. Instead,
the ride was smooth, reminding many passengers of the
motion of a ship at sea. Mark Twain enjoyed his journey to
Nevada immensely, spending the daylight hours stripped to
his drawers and stretched out on the roof of the coach.

The Maidu exhibit is interesting for its rarity. The Maidu
were much less productive than their neighbors, the Mi-
woks. They inhabited a less bounteous region and were
constrained by nature to spend more of their time extracting
the necessities of life from their environment. Accordingly,
they had little time for social development. Their villages
were small and widely scattered in the region of the Sierra
between the Cosumnes River in the south and the Feather
River in the north. Only 8,000 Maidu are believed to have
lived in this vast area prior to 1848, and their numbers
dwindled rapidly after miners invaded their hunting grounds.

A sedentary people, the Maidu seldom traveled more than
one day's journey from their homes. They subsisted largely
on grass seed and acorns ground into a meal in stone mortars
by the women.

The friction was immediate and violent between these
peaceful people and the miners who arrived by the thousands. The newcomers chose the best sites for their own
towns, frequently dispossessing families who had stayed in
the same place for hundreds of years. Placerville and Coloma
both occupy the sites of former villages, as do most of the
other major towns in the golden hills. Miners drove the
Indians away in retaliation for the constant pilferage in
which the latter engaged. More importantly, they slaugh-

Miners at Spanish Flat, c. 1852 *(California State Library)*

tered the deer and other game on which the Indians subsisted, and destroyed with their dams and sluices the streams
in which the Indians fished for salmon. By 1925 only 1,100
Maidu remained alive, and this number would undoubtedly
be smaller had not the Indians been so adept at vanishing into
the countryside whenever posses were formed to hunt them
down.

While at the museum you may want to stay and watch a
film and listen to a lecture on the gold rush. A large grassy
field behind the building provides a perfect setting for a
picnic under the oak trees that border the meadow.

There are other attractions aside from the museum.

Various small exhibits have been set up in gold rush–era buildings nearby, including a mining exhibit complete with a short tunnel. The reconstructed mill is across the highway, and here lectures and demonstrations are also given daily. The mill is a crude structure constructed from untrimmed logs, yet by a quirk of fate this "mill" has become the best-known in the annals of history. Perhaps it is this very randomness of history that so fascinates people: A single moment in time, not very unlike any other moment with which we are familiar, perhaps even this very second, has touched certain people and objects with a kind of immortality. James Marshall was an ordinary man, yet every school-boy and schoolgirl knows his name. The mill is the most rudimentary of all mills and certainly does not deserve the name "building," yet it is as frequently visited as any palace in Europe, and its humble silhouette graces thousands of postcards destined to bear the message "We were here."

It was this very element of chance that drew so many young men to California, to "see the elephant," as they said, to take their ticket in the great lottery of the gold rush. Every man had an equal chance to strike it rich, for gold was distributed haphazardly, scattered by nature into small pockets that enabled one man to prosper while his neighbor went bust.

49ers   The 49ers were mostly young men, sons of middle-class or well-to-do families who could afford their passage to the distant frontier of California. They set out from homes in a spirit of adventure but with no practical knowledge of mining or even of where "Californy" might be. They were frequently well-educated: Dame Shirley's husband came to the camps to ply his trade as a doctor but found his profession useless; there were too many doctors.

Not that sickness was lacking. The 49ers streamed into an area where no white men had lived before. They had no knowledge of the local plants on which the Indians subsisted, and food quickly became a luxury item. Their diet generally consisted of beef jerky and stale bread, though many supple-mented this meager diet with copious amounts of hard liquor. The working conditions were abominable, though the workers had only themselves to blame. In the summer, with temperatures in the river canyons hovering around the

century mark, men worked sixteen hours a day waist-deep
in icy water. Clothing soon wore out, but the miners were so
intent on their work that they paid scant attention to their
own personal well-being. As a result, scurvy, cholera, and
typhus carried off many a miner. Boys who had left comfort-
able homes in the East, where they had never known want,
returned from the goldfields broken old men, their bodies
wracked by malnutrition and disease, with scarcely a rag of
clothing on their backs. Others, of course, became millionaires. It was a great crap shoot, and if the stakes were high,
well, so were the rewards.

A unique way to experience the American River as the   *American River*
49ers did is to take a ride down the river on a rubber raft.
Several rafting companies with offices in Lotus offer one-
and two-day excursions along the American. Most runs begin at Chili Bar and end at Folsom Lake; some offer stops at
historic points along the way. The river trip itself is an
exciting one, with over fifty rapids which have been given
fanciful names like Meatgrinder and Satan's Cesspool.

There are many points of historical interest along the
way. The American was the first river to be fully exploited
by goldseekers. Every bar along the river was dug up, for it
was at those points where the direct flow of the river was
interrupted by sand bars that gold was most frequently discovered. Many of the bars yielded more than a million dollars worth of gold. Bustling settlements grew up overnight
beside these rich diggins, where each man's claim was se-
verely limited to the area he could work by himself—on the
richest bars, a claim might be no more than ten square feet.

Other bars were remembered for events that occurred
near them. Murderer's Bar, located two or three miles   *Murderer's Bar*
upriver from the confluence of the North and Middle Forks
of the American, took its name from the killing of five
miners by Indians in the spring of 1849. The Indians were
actually retaliating for members of their tribe who had been
slain by the whites, but the incident was used as an excuse to
raise a posse and run every Indian out of the goldfields. The
posse found and burned two villages but never caught up
with the culprits.

Rattlesnake Bar was the headquarters of another band of
desperadoes, this one led by the infamous Richard H. Barter,   *Rattlesnake Bar*

Bar Names

What they call a Bar in California is the flat which is usually found on the convex side of a bend in a river. Such places have nearly always proved very rich, that being the side on which any deposit carried down by the river will naturally lodge, while the opposite bank is generally steep and precipitous, and contains little or no gold. Indeed, there are not many exceptions to the rule that, in a spot where one bank of a river affords good diggings, the other side is not worth working.

The largest camps or villages on the rivers are on the bars, and take their names from them.

The nomenclature of the mines is not very choice or elegant. The rivers all retain the names given to them by the Spaniards, but every little creek, flat, and ravine, besides of course the towns and villages which have been called into existence, have received their names at the hands of the first one or two miners who have happened to strike the diggings. The individual pioneer has seldom shown much invention or originality in his choice of a name; in most cases he has either immortalised his own by tacking "ville" or "town" to the end of it, or has more modestly chosen the name of some place in his native State; but a vast number of places have been absurdly named from some trifling incident connected with their first settlement; such as Shirt Tail Cañon, Whisky Gulch, Port Wine Diggins, Humbug Flat, Murderer's Bar, Flapjack Cañon, Yankee Jim's, Jackass Gulch, and hundreds of others with equally ridiculous names.

J. D. Borthwick, *3 Years in California*, 1857

alias Rattlesnake Dick. Dick arrived at the goldfields in 1850 when he was but seventeen years of age. He pursued the life of a miner until 1853, when he was falsely accused of stealing a mule and sentenced to state prison. The real thief was caught before Dick could be incarcerated, but the incident apparently soured him on laws in general.

Soon the golden hills were plagued by a new band of outlaws led by Rattlesnake Dick, the self-styled "pirate of the placers." Although he was apprehended many times, Dick always managed to escape from prison and return to his life of crime. He was finally retired by a bullet in 1859. When he was shot, Dick was wearing a fancy suit and white kid gloves.

Chili Bar (north of Placerville on Highway 193) took its *Chili Bar* name from the Chilean miners who died and were buried in a mass grave there after a smallpox epidemic had wiped out the camp. The Chileans were among the first to arrive at the goldfields, by virtue of the fact that Chile lay on the regular shipping lane around Cape Horn to California. Rumors had already spread through the countryside by the time the first ship bearing gold from California, the *Adelaida*, arrived in Valparaiso on August 29, 1848. Within a month, nearly every ship of Chilean registry was on its way to California carrying men and supplies.

Despite the seemingly extravagant prices charged for some articles of merchandise, not every ship turned a profit. In fact, many of them never returned at all, for their crews deserted in San Francisco and the ships were left to rot in the harbor. By the end of 1849, 92 out of 119 ships of Chilean registry were derelicts in San Francisco Bay. Many of these ships never returned to Chile; instead, they were beached at high tide and used as shops and wharves, or else they were broken up for use as building material.

Even when a ship did manage to depart, its cargo may not have been sold for a profit. Beef jerky, a major export of Chile, became so plentiful that bales of it were used as sidewalks in the city of San Francisco, where the streets were so muddy and filled with potholes that whole jackasses sometimes sank out of sight. Naturally, wood was very expensive: many of the first wooden buildings were brought from China in pieces and reassembled on the site.

Given these conditions of wild fluctuation, when an

article might be found in superabundance one week and
unobtainable at any price the following, shrewd speculators
could make their fortunes with only a small amount of
capital and a few well-stocked warehouses. Collis P. Huntington, who would become one of the richest men in the
country, got the jump on his competitors by rowing out to
the newly arrived ships as they entered the harbor and
buying their cargoes before they had touched land.

PLACERVILLE

The first men to reach the rich diggins around Coloma
were those already resident in California. Thriving cities
like San Francisco and San Jose were turned into ghost towns
overnight as their able-bodied residents answered the call of
gold en masse. Next came the Mexicans from Sonora, many
of whom were already skillful miners who taught the
Yankees how to find gold. The Chileans followed, and they
were followed in turn by the Yankees who came around the
horn on sailing ships. Sometimes the Americans would get
off at Panama and make their way across the Isthmus. Once
they reached the Pacific shore, these would-be miners had to
wait for a ship bound for California that was not already
overloaded with goldseekers. Many of them succumbed to
yellow fever and malaria before a ship arrived.

Finally came the hordes of Americans who had been living
in the Mississippi River valley. They came in covered
wagons drawn by yokes of oxen. The trek might take six
months, for the oxen moved slowly and had to spend many
hours a day browsing on prairie grass. Women and children
found life on the trail especially trying, including the woman
to whom legend bequeathed the name "Sweet Betsy from
Pike." Pike referred to Pike County, Missouri, but generally
a piker was any country boy who had contracted gold fever
and gone to see the elephant. The goal of Betsy, as of every
piker, was Hangtown—now known as Placerville:

> They suddenly stopped on a very high hill
> With wonder looked down on old Placerville

> Ike sighed when he said, as he cast his eyes down
> 'Sweet Betsy, my darling, we've got to Hangtown!'

Placerville does indeed lie at the bottom of a steep ravine (where Highways 49 and 50 cross). The roads winding down to it are said to have been laid out following the path of the mule trains as they zig-zagged slowly down the steep slopes.

During the first year of the gold rush, calm tempers prevailed. Gold was plentiful and there were more claims available than there were people to claim them. In January of 1849, however, the state of affairs changed abruptly. With some miners becoming wealthy and others without the price of a shovel, robberies began to occur, disputes broke out over claims, and vigilante "justice" reared its ugly head.

The first lynching took place in Hangtown and was the source of the name. A mob of angry miners assembled to mete out justice to five petty felons and watched as they were publicly flogged. At this point, a man stepped forward and accused three of those present, a Chilean and two Frenchmen, with attempted murder and robbery. The three were seized and the trial commenced immediately. The three could not defend themselves as they spoke no English, and the charges were found inconclusive, but nevertheless the unfortunate three were adjudged bad characters who deserved to hang. The sentence was carried out, as was generally the case in these affairs, immediately.

Before the ignominious episode of which we have spoken, the place was known as Dry Diggins, or Old Dry Diggins. The town was founded by William Daylor in 1848. By 1854, the citizens had had enough of the name Hangtown, and it was changed to Placerville. In 1857 the county seat was moved from Coloma, where only a few hardy miners remained, to Placerville, which was becoming an important crossroads and supply center. During the 1850s the county had a population of about 20,000 souls, but emigration had reduced this figure to 11,000 by the 1880s.

Placerville thrived during the early boom times. Many businessmen got their start here, including Philip Armour, a butcher who later built up a mid-Western meat-packing empire, and Mark Hopkins, later a railroad magnate. Leland Stanford ran a store in Cold Springs, five miles up the hill,

Sunday in Hangtown

... During the week, and especially when the miners were all at work, Hangtown was comparatively quiet; but on Sundays it was a very different place. On that day the miners living within eight or ten miles all flocked in to buy provisions for the week—to spend their money in the gambling-rooms—to play cards—to get their letters from home—and to refresh themselves, after a week's labour and isolation in the mountains, in enjoying the excitement of the scene according to their tastes.

... The street was crowded all day with miners loafing about from store to store, making their purchases and asking each other to drink, the effects of which began to be seen at an early hour in the number of drunken men, and the consequent frequency of rows and quarrels. Almost every man wore a pistol or knife—many wore both—but they were rarely used. The liberal and prompt administration of Lynch law had done a great deal towards checking the wanton and indiscriminate use of these weapons on any slight occasion. The utmost latitude was allowed in the exercise of self-defence. In the case of a row, it was not necessary to wait till a pistol was actually leveled at one's head—if a man made even a motion towards drawing a weapon, it was considered perfectly justifiable to shoot him first, if possible. The very prevalence of the custom of carrying arms thus in a great measure was a cause of their being seldom used. They were never drawn out of bravado, for when a man once drew his pistol, he had to be prepared to use it, and to use it quickly, or he might expect to be laid low by a ball from his adversary; and again, if he shot a man without sufficient provocation, he was pretty sure of being accommodated with a hempen cravat by Judge Lynch.

J. D. Borthwick, *3 Years in California*, 1857

John M. Studebaker, c. 1903 *(Courtesy, The Covello Collection)*

during the winter of 1852–1853. Cold Springs, once a thriving suburb of Hangtown, now is a ghost town marked only by a cemetery on the hill.

J. M. Studebaker

J. M. Studebaker worked in a shop at 545 Main Street for five years (1853 to 1858) before returning to his home in South Bend, Indiana, with enough money to start a buggy factory. His family's firm began making automobile bodies a generation later. The Studebaker shop is marked by a plaque.

Edwin Markham

Ulysses S. Grant frequently visited the saloons of Hangtown while stationed nearby as a young army officer. Edwin Markham taught school here. Markham has little fame now, but caused a great stir with his poem "Man with a Hoe," a mawkish poem that had Socialist overtones. The popular press, then engaged in a fight against big business in general and the Southern Pacific Railroad in particular, created so much ballyhoo over the poem that Collis P. Huntington offered a $1,000 prize for a poem which would express sentiments contrary to "Man with a Hoe."

Hank Monk

Mark Twain, Horace Greeley, and Hank Monk are three names inextricably bound up with early Placerville on account of a stagecoach ride that took place in 1859. The driver of the coach was Hank Monk, one of the noblemen of the whip who may have served as a model for Bret Harte's fictional hero, Yuba Bill. Monk's chief abilities, however, were daredevil driving and telling lies. He seems to have invented a tall tale for every stop the stage made on the run between Carson City and Placerville, and it was probably his story-telling abilities that kept the tale of that ride alive for years after it took place.

As for the ride itself, nothing much happened, except that Horace Greeley, who was coming west for the first time after urging young men to go west for years in the editorials of his newspaper, made the mistake of admitting he was terrified by the breakneck speed of the stagecoach along the edge of a canyon. Years later, when Greeley became a candidate for president against U. S. Grant, his political enemies resurrected the story in such a way as to make a laughingstock of the newspaper publisher, for they painted him as a cowardly buffoon whose head had made a hole in the roof of the coach.

While writing *Roughing It*, Mark Twain evidently could not resist this humorous incident, only he retold it so that the story itself became the butt of his satirical barbs. Twain claims to have met several strangers on his journey on the Overland Trail by stagecoach, all of whom recited the following story, word for word the same:

> I can tell you a most laughable thing indeed, if you would like to listen to it. Horace Greeley went over this road once. When he was leaving Carson City he told the driver, Hank Monk, that he had an engagement to lecture at Placerville and very anxious to get ment to lecture at Placerville and was very anxious to get through quick. Hank Monk cracked his whip and down in such a terrific way that it jolted the buttons off of Horace's coat, and finally shot his head clear through the roof of the stage, and then he yelled at Hank Monk

and begged him to go easier—said he wasn't in such a hurry as he was awhile ago. But Hank Monk said, "Keep your seat, Horace, and I'll get you there on time"—and you bet he did, too, what was left of him!"

After hearing this story several times, Twain began to lose his patience, until finally he interrupted a ragged tramp who had started to repeat it yet one more time with the following reproof:

> Suffering stranger, proceed at your peril. You see in me the melancholy wreck of a once stalwart and magnificent manhood. What brought me to this? The thing which you are about to tell. Gradually but surely, that tiresome old anecdote has sapped my strength, undermined my constitution, withered my life. Pity my helplessness. Spare me just this once; and tell me about young George Washington and his little hatchet for a change.

Greeley must have felt exactly the same as Twain, for he died before the inauguration of his rival.

After the placers had played out, Placerville remained an *Placerville* important shipping center. The Placerville Road, constructed privately in 1858, carried much of the freight to Virginia City during the heyday of the Comstock Lode (1859 to 1866). After the completion of the transcontinental railroad, its prosperity quickly waned.

Today in Placerville you can see many of the original gold rush structures lining the picturesque main street, as well as a few other oddities. At the west end of town stands Engine No. 1771, the last steam engine retired from the Placerville-Sacramento run. Part way up the street is a monument holding the fire bell rung in the old days to call out the volunteer fire brigade. The site of the original hangman's tree, located at 905 Main Street, is a spot of more than ordinary significance, marking as it does the location of the first American lynching in California.

City government occupies a building constructed in 1860 by an unusual pioneer, a woman, Mary Jane Stroyers-Johnson. A legend in her own right, Mrs. Johnson is said to have driven a herd of cattle across the prairies to form the foundation of her fortune.

Next door is the county courthouse, built in 1912 and flanked by two civil war cannon. The low structure gracefully and unostentatiously symbolizes civic stolidity. Across the street is the Pearson Soda Works, now converted into a restaurant and soda fountain. The first story was built in 1859 and the second, added in 1897, may be reached by a circular wrought-iron stairway. An underground tunnel penetrating 150 feet into the hill behind the building was used for the storage of ice in the days when ice was brought down from the high mountains in winter and stored to provide cooling in the summertime. At the edge of the downtown area stands a monument to the memory of Frederick Sieg, the founder of the first Druid's Grove in California in 1859. On the hill behind the monument, where it was moved from the main street, stands the first Methodist Episcopal Church in California. The lumber used in its construction had to be shipped around the horn in 1851.

Also of interest will be the museum, located at the fairgrounds at the west end of town and the Gold Bug Mine, located in a park at the northeast corner of Placerville. The Gold Bug is open to the public and features a restored stamp mill.

Highway 50—Emigrant Trail

In 1896, Highway 50 became the first State Highway. It had begun as a wagon road in 1858, when convenience rather than speed had become the important factor in western travel. Prior to that time the Carson Pass route to the south had been more heavily traveled, and the Echo Summit route had been known as the Johnson Cut-off. The more northerly route had the advantage of avoiding the steep pitches of the eastern escarpment and making heavy freight traffic more feasible.

During the period of the Comstock Lode, the Placerville Road was the most heavily traveled in the state. Both the Butterfield stage line and the Pony Express used this road, as well as numerous freight wagons, oxcarts and mule trains. For awhile it seemed that the transcontinental railway

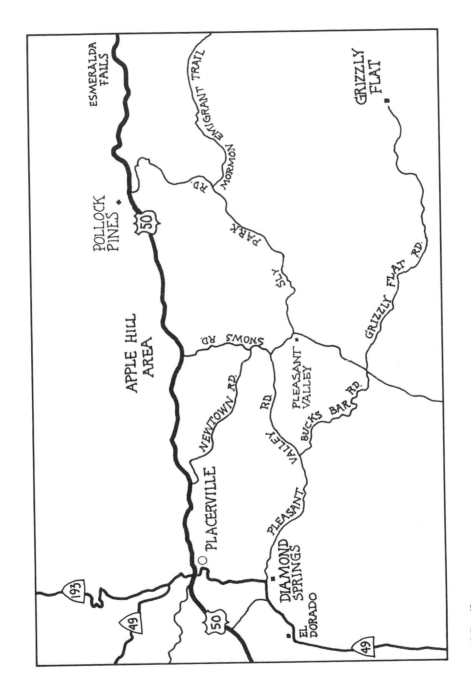

ESMERALDA FALLS

MORMON EMIGRANT TRAIL

GRIZZLY FLAT

50

POLLOCK PINES

SLY PARK RD.

GRIZZLY FLAT RD.

APPLE HILL AREA

SNOW'S RD.

NEWTOWN RD.

PLEASANT VALLEY

PLEASANT VALLEY RD.

BUCKS BAR RD.

PLACERVILLE

193

49

50

PLEASANT

DIAMOND SPRINGS

EL DORADO

49

MAP 3.

would pass this way, but the Sacramento Valley Railroad abandoned its plans and did not reach Placerville until 1888.

Shingle Springs

Shingle Springs was the eastern terminus for the Sacramento Valley Railroad in 1865. It was the site of an early lumber mill that manufactured shingles, as well as of fresh water springs, hence the name. Two miles southeast of Shingle Springs was a settlement called French Creek because it was settled by Frenchmen and French Canadians. The whole community moved to Greenwood after the placers gave out here.

El Dorado

Not far south of Highway 50 is El Dorado, where Highway 49 turns south toward Amador County. El Dorado, originally known as Mud Springs, became the center of a large quartz-mining district. It lies astride the Mother Lode, a network of gold-bearing white quartz veins that runs south to Mariposa and north to Georgetown. El Dorado has several old buildings, including a large stone structure that housed the volunteer fire department.

Diamond Springs

Diamond Springs was another stage stop, noted for its crystal clear water. It had a population of around 1,500 in 1853, but today has only a few sandstone buildings to attract the interest of the wayfarer.

Pleasant Valley

From Diamond Springs you can take the Pleasant Valley Road eastward into the hills where lie the remains of several once-prosperous communities. Pleasant Valley was named by a group of Mormons who stopped there on their way back to Salt Lake City. They found gold here but did not stop long enough to exploit the placers, as they had received orders from Brigham Young to return. The route they followed ran from Pleasant Valley along Sly Park Road to Sly Park Dam Road, where it becomes Mormons Emigrant Trail and heads southwest to join Highway 88 near Silver Basin.

Grizzly Flat

The largest of the mining towns was Grizzly Flat (Pleasant Valley Road to Buck's Bar Road to Grizzly Flat Road), where 1,000 miners hunted their fortunes in 1852. A lumber mill was built in 1856 to provide much-needed boards for the miners. During the 1880s there were several hydraulic operations in the vicinity and a few quartz mines as well.

Apple Hill

Highway 50 continues on past Placerville through a rich fruit-growing district known as Apple Hill. The mountain varieties of apples and pears are smaller than those grown in

Grizzly Flat, c. 1849 *(Courtesy, The Bancroft Library)*

the lower elevations, but many believe them superior in taste and overall quality. Apples begin ripening toward the end of summer, when some ranchers permit visitors to pick their own fruit. Other fruits are grown in the area as well, including peaches and plums. Delicious fresh apple cider and apple pies are also sold in some locations.

Not far from the entrance to El Dorado National Forest (just east of Pollock Pines) is Esmeralda Falls, an early landmark. Along the road you will see the stone markers used to measure the distance from Placerville on the original state highway. One of the most picturesque way stations was located at Sayles Flat, in the shadow of Lover's Leap—which incidentally received its name from a story of dubious authenticity that Hank Monk was fond of telling his passengers.

Esmeralda Falls

Rising to the north of the highway past Strawberry is Ralston Peak, a 9,000-foot mountain that was named for the great tycoon of early San Francisco, Billy Ralston. Together with Darius Ogden Mills, Ralston founded the Bank of California and proceeded to develop the state as rapidly as he could. His development of the Comstock Lode mines and his ownership of the railroad there brought him great riches,

Ralston Peak

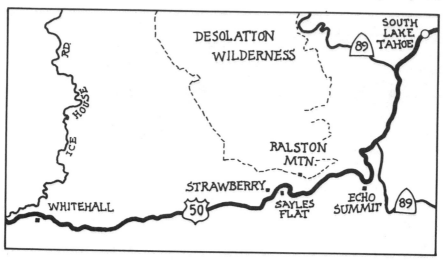

MAP 4.

Desolation
Wilderness

but he risked his investors' money unwisely and ended up a bankrupt and (almost certainly) a suicide in 1875.

Ralston Peak marks the southern boundary of Desolation Wilderness, a region in which no motor vehicles are allowed and all refuse must be packed out. Here the Sierra is truly wild, and the hardy adventurer may watch nature's daily spectacle in all its primeval glory. Inaccessible in winter, the region has chill weather even in the summertime. The topography consists of sheer granite cliffs and crystal clear lakes. Snow lingers all year round in the shadows of the higher peaks and summer nights are chill.

The rare atmosphere has a rejuvenating effect on the senses: Distant peaks seem to loom directly above you and contrasts between bright sunlight and deep shadow are dramatic; the aroma of pine permeates the air, while the smoke from a single campfire can be smelled for miles. Sounds, too, are more noticeable, especially in the absence of electric motors and automobile engines—the breezes rushing through the trees sound like the waves of the ocean pounding on a far-off beach. Once you have seen the stars on a bright summer's night, you will never forget the spectacle. No wonder so many people make an annual pilgrimage to the high Sierra, and even those who don't have worked hard for the preservation of this aboriginal wilderness area.

Past Echo Summit the highway follows the course of the Upper Truckee River to Lake Tahoe, the jewel of the Sierra.

Placerville Area—Georgetown Loop

The Cold Springs Road leads through Gold Hill northwest from Placerville. The area had numerous mining camps in the early days. The most remarkable settlers on Gold Hill were Japanese farmers imported from their native country to work at the Wakamatsu colony. The enterprise was started by T. H. Schnell, a native of Germany who had lived most of his life in Japan. Schnell noticed the similarity of terrain and climate between Gold Hill and parts of Japan where tea and silk were cultivated. The land was cheap and Schnell was ambitious, so he commenced his farm in 1868 with a few Japanese farmhands, making this the earliest Japanese settlement in America.

Gold Hill

Schnell planned to raise tea, flax, Japanese wax trees, and mulberry bushes—the latter to be used for the production of silk moths. Sixteen more Japanese arrived in 1869, and by the following year there were 150,000 tea plants. The colony was short-lived, however. Problems developed when miners began prospecting for gold on the cultivated grounds, and when tea plants, evidently not of the best quality, did not produce expected yields, Schnell journeyed to Japan to raise more capital and was reportedly killed before he could return.

A mile north of Coloma along Highway 49 is Lotus, originally called Marshall and later known as Uniontown. An early ferry across the American River was replaced by a bridge that netted its owners $600 to $800 a month in the early 1850s.

Lotus

The huge house at Pilot Hill (six miles from Coloma) was originally a hotel, built by Alcandor Bayley in 1862. Bayley intended to be the first to get rich when the Sacramento Valley Railroad extended its line into the state of Nevada, but the railroad went through Auburn instead and the hotel remains as a monument to man's foolish ambitions. The site to the left of the house was formerly occupied by the barn in which the first Grange Hall in California was organized in 1870 by Bayley and local farmers. By 1860 wheat had be-

Pilot Hill

come the most important product in California, surpassing gold in dollar value. The true value of the gold rush lay not in its production of metallic wealth, however, but in the huge impetus it provided for economic growth. Developments that would have taken generations to accomplish under normal conditions were accelerated by the discovery of gold so that they took only a few years or a decade.

Cool

Cool was once a stage stop, although it does little more now than mark the junction of 49 with Highway 193, which passes through Greenwood and Georgetown to the east.

Greenwood

Greenwood has the air of a town where something once happened. Situated in a quiet vale, this town took its name from one of the most colorful of all California characters, Caleb Greenwood—or perhaps from his son John, for the Greenwoods traveled together and the clan had many members. John was a hell-raiser who ran a general store here briefly in 1848 before being force to flee the area on account of his habit of taking potshots at peaceful Indians. He was later killed in a gambling dispute.

Caleb Greenwood was born, by some accounts, in 1763. He was the guide on the Donner Party crossing in 1846 and later started the famous Gold Lakes hoaxes. His record was none too good, but may be excused by the fact that he was already eighty-one by the time he arrived in California for the first time. Besides John, he had at least two other sons, one of whom settled near Bolinas in Marin County. Caleb himself died during the winter of 1849–1850.

John A. Stone

Another renowned resident of Greenwood was John A. Stone, whose remains lie in the cemetery here. Better known as Old Put, Stone had a genius for satire. His *California Songster*, a collection of satiric songs published in 1854, sold 25,000 copies. Stone's songs often reflected the reality of a miner's life better than the accounts of men who sought to publicize its virtues and soft-pedal its faults. He lampooned miners who pretended to be honest while they made a living by petty thievery:

> No matter who was robbed or killed, 'twas all laid to Joaquin,
> His band out in the chapparal not long ago was seen;

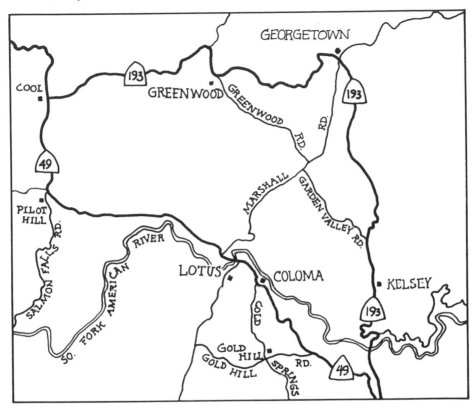

MAP 5.

With pick and shovel on his back, as though out on a
    tramp,
An honest miner might have been seen, robbing a
    Chinese Camp.

Here we can see how some miners took advantage of a viru-
lent anti-Mexican sentiment to cover their own crimes—
incidentally explaining how so many crimes came to be
ascribed to Joaquin Murieta.

In another of his poems, Old Put made fun of the sentimental ideal popularized by Bret Harte in "Tennessee's
Partner":

When I was mining with my partner
He and I could not agree

I made all the bread, did this that and t'other
He got mad if he had to make the tea.

Apparently the ideal partnership is just as rare as the ideal
marriage.

Georgetown

Greenwood never prospered as its founders had hoped it
would. Instead Georgetown was destined to be the center of
commerce for this district. The reason for this is not hard to
find: Georgetown is situated at the northern end of the
Mother Lode and surrounded by a number of lode mines that
kept on producing long after the surface placers gave out.
There is some confusion as to the origin of the name, for
more than one man named George was associated with the
founding of a town here. The name Growlersburg has sometimes been applied to the diggins, on account of the growl-
ing noise made by the large gold nuggets as the miners
washed their paydirt in the tin pans used for the purpose.

In reference to these gold pans, it should be noted that
very little gold can be extracted from a claim by this method
alone. Modern gold miners (and there are a few) use motorized sluices or doodlebugs which process gold-bearing gravel
in the same way that large gold dredges do. The gravel at the
bottom of a stream is sucked up by a vacuum hose and
washed automatically, with the worthless gravel and sand
being returned to the stream.

This method works well enough, though it mostly depends on finding a site where few dredges have been operated recently so that gold washed down from the mountains
will have had a chance to accumulate. Some miners use scuba
gear to vacuum the bottoms of reservoirs and small ponds;
others hike into isolated regions far from the nearest road.
Many miners claim to have made a lot of money during the
recent drought years, when reservoirs were reduced to a
trickle and areas usually covered by many fathoms of water
were exposed for dredging.

Whatever the truth of this or any other gold-mining tale,
the miner's pan is not sufficient in itself for anything but
prospecting in the purest sense, or for washing out the
paydirt that has accumulated in a sluice during the course of
a day. The pan may profitably be used as well for a peculiar
process known as pocket mining, at which many 49ers were

Panning out (*Charles Nordhoff's* California)

able to make a living long after the gold rush was over.

The principle of pocket mining is simple. In the Mother Lode region, gold frequently occurred in pockets rather than veins, which accounts for the fact that a man might prosper while neighboring claims produced nothing. Assuming that a pocket exists somewhere up the slope from a stream, a prospector could find its location by panning the sand in the stream until he found color, a few grains of gold. Then he proceeded along the stream, prospecting every few feet, until the color disappeared. He continued this process, moving slowly up the slope, until he had found the pocket, which would generally be located at the apex of a triangle. This process was long and laborious, but pockets could pay off their lucky discoverer with thousands of dollars worth of gold.

Georgetown had placer deposits, too, and rich ones. By 1854, the community could boast 3,000 residents. Quartz mines like the Argonaut, Black Oak, and Cove Hill kept the town alive for many years. The main street is 100 feet wide and runs along the divide between the South Fork and the Middle Fork of the American River. This area was extremely rich in gold. The Middle Fork was the richest river in the state, with a total production of more than a hundred million dollars of gold at twelve dollars an ounce. Several individual bars had productions ranging from one to three million dollars.

In places far from any river, so-called dry diggins like Placerville and Georgetown, it was necessary to bring water in by the cartload. This was a costly process, with prices ranging up to a dollar a gallon.

Soon companies were formed to construct aqueducts, called sluices or flumes, to bring water to dry diggins from dams in the mountains. The water was brought in ditches except where flumes had to be constructed to carry it across canyons. By 1855 more than 600 miles of ditches had been dug in El Dorado County alone at a cost of over a million dollars.

Kelsey   Highway 193 turns south at Georgetown toward Kelsey, another early gold-mining town. Named after its founder, Benjamin Kelsey, this was the first dry diggins in the state. A flood of emigrants arrived here during 1849, with each nationality setting up its own camp, as was the custom during the gold rush. The names of the camps give a clue to the nationality of their residents: Louisville was French; Irish Creek, Irish; Elizatown, English; American Flat, American; and Spanish Flat, either Mexican or Chilean, or both. There was also a Fleatown in the vicinity, though its name give no clue to its nationality—all miners were afflicted by what they called "the fierce, sanguinary flea."

Kelsey is best remembered as the place where James Marshall lived from 1870 until his death at age seventy-three in 1885. His blacksmith shop can be seen today.

Part Two:

Sacramento to Tahoe—Over the Hump on Interstate 80

When John Sutter received a land grant of eleven Spanish leagues (seventy-six square miles) from the Mexican governor of California, he dreamed of setting up a private fiefdom in the western wilds. The grant was "floating," which meant that the land could be located anywhere within certain broad boundaries. In 1839 the entire Sacramento Valley lay vacant except for Indians and wildlife. In August of that year Sutter began work on a fortress that was to be the key to his kingdom.

Sutter's Fort, at 2701 L Street, is today surrounded by a large city, the city that gold built. Its location proved as crucial as Sutter had hoped, and it is now the capital of the state. Not much else went according to plan.

Sutter's Fort

The original fort was stripped of all its furnishings by the 49ers, but has been reconstructed to approximate its condition before their arrival. Here you can see the shops and living quarters that made up an early California rancho—except for his walls and cannon, Sutter was no different from dozens of other Spanish land barons.

Soon after the discovery of gold, a boomtown grew on the mud flats at the confluence of the Sacramento and American rivers. The location of this boomtown was at Front and J streets, today within the confines of Old Sacramento. The town consisted of merchants' stalls thrown up in confusion by the water's edge. There were no property owners, nor any

Old Sacramento

licenses to sell: A man became a merchant if he had something to sell; he became a shopkeeper by finding a vacant spot of land, placing his merchandise on it, and shouting at the top of his lungs whenever a potential buyer came within earshot. Here was the marketplace at its freest, the West at its wildest, and human nature in its rawest form. Fortunes were made and lost overnight. Sutter was soon ruined by more skillful competitors, and Sam Brannan, for a while the most prosperous man in California, lost his fortune to land speculators and cardsharps.

The spirit of gambling was in the air. There were thousands of monte banks in the state, but here again the private individual had a free hand. The typical monte bank was a crate set up by some person who had come into possession of a few ounces of gold and wanted to further increase his stake by playing cards instead of working. Monte was the favorite game because it was fast and required no skill. One card was dealt to each player, who then wagered according to his fancy, and the highest card took the pot. The game offered an unbelievable opportunity to anyone who could palm a card or deal the second card from the top of the deck.

The spirit of gambling was not limited, however, to the casinos or the gaming tables. In the business world, rash speculation carried the day. Brannan made a killing by cornering the market in mining pans. Huntington and Hopkins later accomplished the same feat with shovels and blasting powder. The biggest gamble of them all was the transcontinental railroad.

Railway Museum

The Sacramento terminus of the Southern Pacific has been converted into a railway museum. Located on Front Street between I and J, this museum represents an extraordinary collection of locomotives and cars that once rode the rails over the hump.

Across the mud flat from the railroad museum is the tiny Eagle Theater. The present structure is a faithful reconstruction of the original, one of the first permanent structures in Sacramento—though permanent may not be the right word, since the theater was washed away by the flood of 1850. The miners craved diversion, whether at the gaming tables or at public performances. Many acting troupes toured California during the first few years, for ticket prices

An early view of Sutter's Fort (*Courtesy, The Covello Collection*)

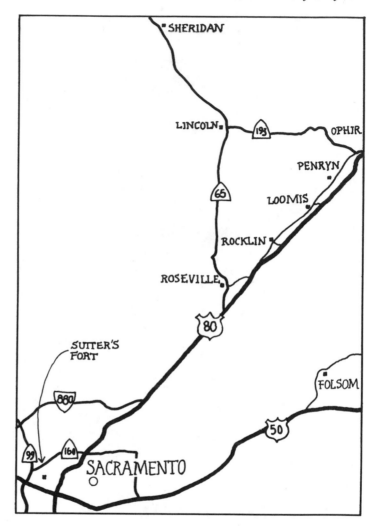

MAP 6.

were high and miners were accustomed to showering the stage with gold when they particularly approved of a performance. Today, the Old Eagle Theater presents old-time melodramas and re-enactments of such historic events as the Donner tragedy.

As the years passed, Sacramento grew away from the waterfront. Collis Huntington and Mark Hopkins went into partnership in a large hardware store on K Street—the same store in which Crazy Judah called together the merchants of

Sacramento in a Rush

The road to Sutter's Fort, the main streets, and
the levee fronting on the Embarcadero were con-
stantly thronged with the teams of emigrants, coming in from the mountains. Such worn, weather-
beaten individuals I never before imagined. Their
tents were pitched by hundreds in the thickets
around the town, where they rested a few days
before starting to winter in the mines and elsewhere. At times the levee was filled throughout its
whole length by their teams, three or four yoke of
oxen to every wagon. The beasts had an expression
of patient experience which plainly showed that no
roads yet to be traveled would astonish them in the
least. After tugging the wagons for six months over
the salt deserts of the Great Basin, climbing passes
and canons of terrible asperity in the Sierra Nevada,
and learning to digest oak bark on the arid plains
around the sink of Humboldt's River, it seemed as if
no extremity could henceforth intimidate them.
Much toil and suffering had given to their coun-
tenances a look of almost human wisdom. If their
souls should hereafter, according to the theory of
some modern philosophers, reappear in human
frames, what a crowd of grave and reverend sages
may not California be able to produce! The cows
had been yoked in with the oxen and made to do
equal duty. The women who had come by the overland route appeared to have stood the hardships of
the journey remarkably well, and were not half so
loud as the men in their complaints.

Bayard Taylor
Eldorado: or Adventures in the Path of Empire, 1850

Sacramento to help launch his railroad. Leland Stanford had a wholesale grocery business here, while Charlie Crocker had tried his hand at just about everything. Having failed as a miner, he started driving freight teams between Sacramento and Placerville; later he opened a dry goods store.

Charles Crocker

Crocker was a large, stout man with a no-nonsense temperament. Although he had no construction experience, it was he who managed the building of the Central Pacific. He saw to everything personally, including the payment of the workers. While Stanford sprinkled his speeches with homilies about the solid virtues of industry, thrift, sobriety, and piety, Crocker saw the world from a different perspective. Thrift and sobriety were not enough: one man might work all his life and wind up with nothing, while another, no better than himself, became a millionaire.

When the Civil War caused a labor shortage in California, Crocker suggested the use of Chinese laborers. After some hesitation on the part of the other directors, his proposal was adopted. The Chinese turned out to be marvelous workmen, but Crocker's hiring of them won him no friends among California workingmen. They called the Chinese "Crocker's pets" and feared they would drive wages down by working cheaply.

Whoever did the job, it was a difficult one. The crossing of the Sierra took five years and cost many lives. Most of the earth was moved in wheelbarrows, one load at a time. For blasting tunnels through solid rock, only hand-held drills and blasting powder were used. Dynamite became available in 1866, but its use was abandoned after a few accidents had cost several Chinese lives. Similarly, the steam drill was invented during the period of construction, and its use would have saved weeks or even months of effort. Stanford, who admired every new invention, strongly favored the new drills, but Crocker preferred the old methods and refused to permit its use. Perhaps he was swayed by his experience with dynamite.

Collis Huntington

Huntington was the money man who worked in New York while his long-time partner Hopkins managed the Sacramento end of the business. From the beginning Huntington became deeply involved in politics, making certain that representatives favorable to the railroad were sent to

Washington. If an anti-railroader happened to be elected in California, Huntington could manage that, too, only it cost a bit more.

Stanford, who was elected governor shortly after the railroad was organized, was front man for the group. Although nominally the president of the railroad, he concerned himself little with its actual operation.

Leland Stanford

Before leaving Sacramento, you should pay a visit to the Adams Express Building, the western terminus of the Pony Express, located at the entrance to Old Sacramento. In front of the building is a statue of a rider spurring his horse the final fifty yards, probably the finest piece of sculpture in the gold region. The mail was carried from here to San Francisco by steamboat.

Adams Express Building

Upstairs from the express office is the Supreme Court, which has been reconstructed to form a fine display of early jurisprudence in the state. A kind of aura hangs over the courtroom, while the chambers of the justices retain a sort of refined clubbiness. This and all the other buildings in Old Sacramento have only recently been reclaimed from the status of slums. Whether this kind of urban renewal could be successful in other, less historic areas is questionable, but it certainly represents a great improvement here.

Highway 80 is of course a major freeway today, but it was not much used before the coming of the railroad. Most of the towns along its route are connected with the railway in some way, and it is for this reason that I have begun with a discussion of the Central Pacific and its directors. The Railroad Museum in Old Sacramento is particularly exciting when seen against the backdrop of the momentous struggle of man against nature to link the Eastern states and California with bands of steel. As Oscar Lewis put it in *The Big Four*, "'California Annexes the United States' read the slogan of the day" when the Golden State "half-playful, half-arrogant, prepared to take its place (near the head of the table) with the family of states."

Highway 80

Not far from Sacramento, and just inside Placer County, you will find Roseville. Not an old town, Roseville owes its existence to the railroad. The origin of its name is unknown; it was originally known simply as the Junction, for it was here that the California Central Railroad branched north

Roseville

while the Central Pacific headed northeast toward the foothills. In 1872, Roseville polled only 171 votes. Soon after, in 1876, it was the scene of the murder of three members of the same family by Ah Sam, their Chinese cook. The motive was theft, and the murderer was soon apprehended. Nevertheless, the crime served to intensify anti-Oriental feelings in the area, and all Chinese were forced to leave Roseville, Rocklin, Loomis, and Penryn.

Lincoln

In 1906 the decision was made to move the Southern Pacific Railroad Yards to Roseville, and the town boomed, overnight becoming a major employer of skilled mechanics. The yard had formerly been located at Lincoln, eleven miles north on Highway 65, and resulted in a corresponding decline for the latter town. Lincoln was named for Charles Lincoln Wilson, builder of the California Central, which reached here in 1861, though the fact that a man of the same name had recently become president surely affected the decision. Lincoln was the center of a mineral-producing district whose products included coal and a fine white kaolin clay.

Sheridan

E. C. Rogers settled in the vicinity of Sheridan, a small town eight miles north of Lincoln on Highway 65, about 1857. Two years later he built the "Union Shed" at the crossroads a half-mile south of the present town of Sheridan. Here, four roads converged, from Nicolaus, Auburn, Grass Valley, and Marysville. Rogers ran a wayside inn with a 150-foot shed in front to protect freight teams from the sun. Feeding the livestock provided local farmers with a market for their hay and grain, and so a town was born. It was renamed Sheridan after the great Union general of Civil War fame. The town's location on the Oregon Railroad made it an important shipping center until it was destroyed by disastrous fires in 1866 and 1868. Mark Hopkins chose this location for a flour mill in 1870.

Manzanita Grove

Prosperity brought highwaymen, and these outlaws had a hide-out at Manzanita Grove, a wooded knoll midway between Lincoln and Sheridan. They used the dense forest and underbrush as a natural corral for rustled stock during the 1850s. Today the site of a pioneer cemetery, Manzanita Grove can be reached by means of Chamberlain Road, four miles north of Lincoln along Highway 65. Manzanita Cemetery lies about three miles off the highway, although the knoll itself is visible from the road, only a half-mile to the east.

The Roseville area is currently experiencing a growth spurt that may eventually dwarf the one occasioned by the railroad yard in 1906, for some of the semiconductor firms headquartered in the Santa Clara Valley have chosen to build assembly plants here. The repercussions of this move are far-reaching, for the high-technology industry of Santa Clara and its neighbors in Silicon Valley have almost completely destroyed the agricultural production of the Santa Clara Valley and now threaten to work the same trick in California's Central Valley. The influx of such firms into the Roseville area presents a serious problem for urban planners, especially since urban sprawl in Sacramento has already become dangerous to the rural economy of this part of the state.

Rocklin

Rocklin, once the location of the roundhouse and railroad shops of the Central Pacific Railroad, was founded in 1866. There are many granite quarries in the vicinity, and some of the stone from these quarries can be seen in the state Capitol building's walls. In 1908 the railroad yards here were consolidated with those in Roseville. North of the town lies the estate of J. Parker Whitney, who built an English-style manor house and raised sheep on his 22,000 acres. Whitney, a gentleman farmer in the best sense of the word, produced the first raisins in the state.

Loomis

Loomis was no more than a whistle stop until 1885. Originally named Pino, its mail kept getting confused with that bound for Reno, Nevada, so the name of the town was changed. Jim Loomis was the whole town for many years, acting as a railroad agent, express agent and postmaster. English colonists settled here, too. The whole town was rebuilt after a fire in 1915.

Penryn

Penryn, also noted for its quarries, was founded by the Welshman Griffith Griffith around 1864. Its granite was used in the base of the state Capitol as well as in the U.S. Mint at San Francisco. A granite store was built here in 1878 during a slack period in order to keep the quarries going. Now the center of a rich fruit-growing district, it produces peaches, plums, cherries, and pears. A citrus colony was

Miners in Auburn Ravine, c. 1852 *(California State Library)*

founded here in 1890 by J. Parker Whitney, and most of the settlers in the region were English gentlemen. Named for Griffith's home town of Penrhyn in Wales, Penryn was given its present spelling by an officer of the Central Pacific Railroad who inadvertently struck out the "h."

Ophir   Another important gold rush town, located to the west of Auburn in Auburn Ravine, is Ophir. In 1852 it was the largest town in the county. Between 1875 and 1885 it was the center for quartz mining in Placer County.

Auburn

The area around Auburn was rich in placer deposits, hence you will find many former gold camps here. Sometimes, rarely, the gold camp has been absorbed by a larger town, like Auburn. More frequently, the camp prospered for a while, then perished completely. In those instances, no more than a small unkept cemetery may remain of what once was a "Roaring Camp."

Auburn itself began as one of a dozen similar camps. Gold was discovered here by Claude Chana in the early summer of 1848. Another nearby camp was at Secret Ravine, now Newcastle, two miles west. A large statue of Chana kneeling with his gold pan has become the symbol of Auburn's Old Town.

There is another claimant to the honor of first discovering gold at Auburn, though. John S. Wood was also in the area at that time, and the place came to be known as Wood's Dry Diggins, or North Fork Dry Diggins, from its location on the North Fork of the American River.

The first settlers were members of Colonel Stephenson's New York Regiment. This regiment had fought in Mexico during the war that gave the United States sovereignty over California and the rest of the Southwest. The New York regiment was mustered out of the army in California so that they might form a nucleus for an American community here. It is perhaps for this reason that you will find the names of so many Yankees on the earliest headstones.

The policy of the government, however, had dire consequences for the state after the gold rush. For about a decade there existed an undeclared state of civil war between the Americans, most of them battle-hardened veterans, and the Mexicans (or any other Spanish-speaking nationality). Much of the violence of the early years stems from this source.

During the first year after gold was discovered, there was little violence and hardly any crime. Gold was plentiful and the pace was slow. The tremendous influx of 1849 brought with it competition, race hatred, and finally open warfare.

The first to suffer the consequences of this increased violence in the Auburn area were the Indians. Although not warlike and hostile like their fellow Americans to the east, the Maidu had a marked predilection toward petty thievery. During the summer of 1849 several thefts of liquor, mules, and similar items led to the formation of the California Blades, a vigilante group with twenty-one members who made it their goal to rid the goldfields of Indians. They destroyed an Indian village five miles west of Illinoistown (Colfax) and killed two men at another camp. This was the beginning of a reign of terror that would last until the following June. One robbery was avenged by the death of

twenty Indians whose scalps were hung in front of the
wayside houses between Illinoistown and Auburn. It need
hardly be emphasized that the practice of taking an enemy's
scalp was introduced into California by the white men.

The narrow divide between the North and Middle forks
of the American River was exceptionally rich in placer gold.
Yankee Jim's, Todd's Valley, Wisconsin Hill, and Iowa Hill
were all early camps with large mining populations. Iowa
Hill alone yielded $100,000 per week in 1856—after hydraul-
ic mining had been developed. Several large nuggets were
reported in 1849 and 1850, two of them weighing more than
twenty-five pounds.

The area northwest of Todd's Valley formed part of the
Big Blue Lead, a deposit of gold in ancient river gravels that
rivaled the mother lode itself in richness. The gravel beds
were a hundred feet deep, but the gold was very thinly
dispersed in them and large waterworks, including canals,
dams, flumes, and sluices, had to be built in order to exploit
the deposits. By 1855, Placer County already had twenty-
nine canals totaling 480 miles in length. More were built
later.

Auburn did not owe its growth to the richness of the gold
deposits there, but to its location at the confluence of the
North and Middle forks of the American. The divide between the American and Bear rivers is narrow and the
canyons on either side are deep. The route followed by
Interstate 80 is the only possible outlet for this region. In
addition, the crossing of the American near Auburn is the
shortest route to Placerville and the Southern Mines, while
the route to Grass Valley and the Northern Mines is direct
and easy. In fact, Auburn always occupied the central
position between the northern and southern mines, even
when Placerville had more traffic over the mountains to
Nevada.

In this world of stage coaches and freight wagons, two
types of humanity stood out from the rest. One was "the
original and fanatical tyrant of the brotherhood of Jehu, the
stage driver, the other, the bold bandit." The stage driver
has been frequently depicted in prose.

Mark Twain described the stage-driver as a great per-
sonage:

In the eyes of the station-keeper and the hostler, the stage-driver was a hero—a great and shining dignitary, the world's favorite son ... When they spoke to him they received his insolent silence meekly, and as being the natural and proper conduct of so great a man; when he opened his lips they all hung on his words with admiration (he never honored a particular individual with a remark, but addressed it with a broad generality to the horses, the stables, the surrounding country *and* the human underlings); ... How admiringly they would gaze up at him in his high seat as he gloved himself with lingering deliberation, while some happy hostler held the bunch of reins aloft, and waited patiently for him to take it!

Bret Harte made the stage-driver a figure in many of his tales. Yuba Bill, the driver, generally appeared at the beginning or the end of a story. He was the one who introduced men to the adventurous life of the goldfields, and ushered them back to the world of hum-drum existence. Yuba was gruff, laconic, and scornful of civilization. The particular butt of his coarse humor was the tenderfoot, as for instance, the passenger who claimed there must be no tree blocking the road because he couldn't see it. "Now, that's onfortnit!" said Yuba Bill grimly; "but ef any gentleman will only lend him an opery glass, mebbe he can see round the curve and over the other side o' the hill where it is."

Such was the kind of man who drove the concord stages over the narrow mountain tracks and contended with all the obstacles that nature and desperate men could provide.

On the other hand, there were the outlaws. Actually, these men were more interesting and varied than their law-abiding adversaries. The most famous outlaws in the golden hills were heads of outlaw bands that terrorized the entire region. Joaquin Murieta, called the Robin Hood of the Placers, became a culture hero for the Mexicans and Spanish-speaking Californians. Like many another outlaw, he was portrayed as driven to a life of crime by injustice. Charles Bolton, better known to posterity as Black Bart, led a double life. A gentleman in San Francisco society, he became an outlaw along the highways of the Mother Lode. Handsome,

Black Bart

Charles E. Bolton, a.k.a. Black Bart *(Courtesy, The Covello Collection)*

literate, and popular, Bolton served a short prison term, then disappeared from California for good—some claim that Wells Fargo paid him a pension to stop robbing their stages!

In 1850, California was divided into twenty-seven counties. At that time, Auburn was included in Sutter County, of which Oroville was the county seat. In the following year, a special election was held to determine the county seat of a new county, called Placer. Auburn won an election in which more votes were cast than the total population of the county.

An early census will give an idea of the general make-up of frontier society. In 1852 the total population of the county was 10,784, of which 6,602 were white males and only 343 were white females. The Chinese numbered 3,019, probably all male, while there were 730 Indians.

Although forming only a small minority of the population, women played an important civilizing role and were widely respected in the community. One early female settler was Mary Fee Shannon, who came West with her husband, the editor of the *Placer Democrat*. Mrs. Shannon gained wide popularity as a poetess with the pen-name of Eulalie before dying in childbirth in 1854. She was only thirty years old.

Mary Fee Shannon

Auburn experienced fewer reverses than many of the other mining towns. Her placers gave out at about the same time hydraulic mining was becoming a major industry. As a major crossroads town after the railroad arrived, Auburn was able to weather the abandonment of hydraulic mining. The railroad brought in settlers who used it to ship fruits and livestock to markets in the East.

The courthouse is one of the most dramatic structures in the Mother Lode. Perched on a prominent hill, it is a massive structure constructed of granite from Rocklin and bricks from Lincoln. Built in 1894, it represents the prosperity brought to the region by the railroad.

The same year saw the construction of the Odd Fellows Hall, while the Opera House, an impressive structure seating 700, had been built in 1890. By 1906 a new town had to be opened, called East Auburn, for the town had outgrown its original location in the restrictive confines of Auburn Ravine. This change of location proved fortunate for modern visitors, for many of the building in Old Town have been preserved intact. Today it is a small complex of shops and restaurants that make a pleasant stopping place.

Highway 49 South From Auburn

Not far from Auburn you will arrive at the North Fork of the American River, which winds its way through a large and rugged chasm. This river is a favorite among swimmers and picnickers from as far away as the Bay Area. Unfortunately, it is soon to be inundated by the waters behind Auburn Dam. The highway climbs rapidly on the other side of the canyon heading toward Georgetown, Coloma, and Placerville.

Forest Hill and Michigan Bluff

The Forest Hill Road from Auburn will take you over the North Fork of the American onto the Divide. This was a rich placer area with many camps. One of the most prosperous of these was Yankee Jim's (northwest of Forest Hill on the Colfax Forest Hill Road), noted throughout the state for its richness. It was founded in 1850 by a man named Robinson, who was hanged the following year for horse-stealing. Fruit trees were planted here by a Colonel McClure as early as 1851. Another early resident was Colonel E. D. Baker, who is credited with importing the first bees into the county. He

Yankee Jim's   returned to Yankee Jim's as a congressional candidate in 1859 and went on to become the senator from Oregon. Baker served in the Civil War and died in action at Ball's Bluff.

Todd's Valley   Although founded in 1849, Todd's Valley did not begin to grow until after 1852, when rich mines were discovered in the area. It had an Odd Fellows Hall and a Masonic Lodge. Dr. Todd kept a store and hotel here.

Forest Hill   The only town of any size on the divide today is Forest Hill. One of the hydraulic mining centers, its main street is 200 feet wide. The Forest Hill bell weighs four tons and was cast around 1860.

Michigan Bluff   Michigan Bluff (three miles southeast off Forest Hill Road) was a center for hydraulic mines, some of which may

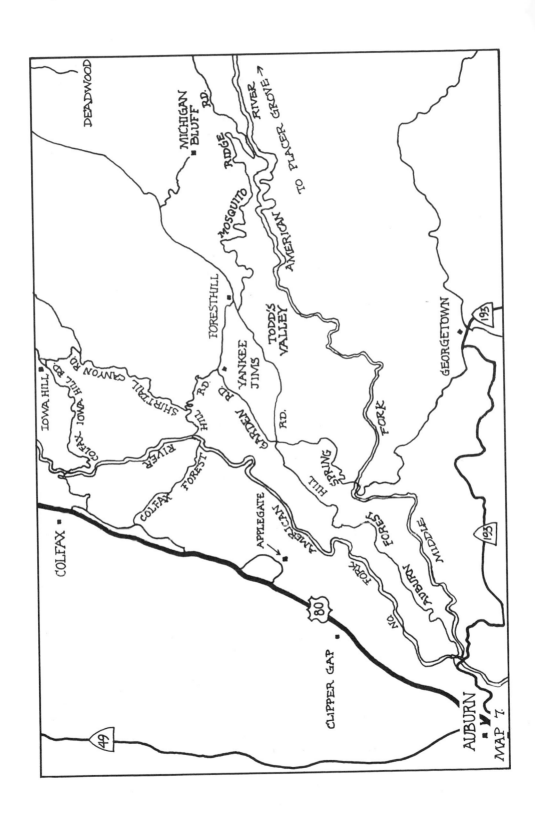

MAP 7.

be seen in the neighborhood. First located at the bottom of the hill, the town was moved to the top in 1857. Leland Stanford had a dry goods store here.

Deadwood

Seven miles from Michigan Bluff (by foot trail) is the ghost town of Deadwood, where Benjamin Colt, inventor of the Colt revolver, is said to have prospected. In those days, "deadwood" meant "a sure thing."

Placer Grove

To the southeast of Deadwood, nestled among the nearly inaccessible canyons feeding into the American, stands the Placer grove of Big Trees, perhaps the least frequently visited of all the Sierra groves. Only a few trees are growing here in the northernmost grove. It can be reached by a twisty drive on Mosquito Ridge Road.

Iowa Hill

Shirttail Canyon Road between Colfax and Forest Hill leads to Iowa Hill. In 1857 there were 600 voters registered here, most of them employed in one or another of the numerous mines. Among the residents was Anna Catharine Markham, wife of the poet Edwin Markham. She was born here and later taught school.

Auburn Region—Interstate 80

Clipper Gap

Leaving Auburn to the northeast on I-80 you will come to Clipper Gap, where an old road left to Yankee Jim's and Forest Hill. This was the site of a Lime Kiln in 1854 and a wayside inn called the Grizzly Bear House, famous as a rendezvous for highwaymen. A large lime rock, visible across the river from the Grizzly Bear House, was the spot where a confederate of the gang, a woman, would light a signal lamp to let the bandits know when a stage was coming up the hill from Forest Hill.

Applegate

Another limekiln was located at Applegate, founded in 1849 and known as Lisbon in the early days. Three-fourths of the lime used to build Sacramento came from Placer County. Applegate was also the site of an esoteric community in the early 1900s. The esoteric movement was a quasi-religious group akin to spiritualism. Followers of men like Ouspensky and Gurdjieff, the esoterics were intellectuals who published many works, including books and pamphlets that originated here in Applegate.

Forest Hill *(Courtesy, The Bancroft Library)*

Colfax

Colfax was above the Placer deposits and in fact was not founded until 1865, when the Central Pacific Railroad reached here. It was called Illinoistown at first, but the name was changed to Colfax when Grant's running mate, Schuyler Colfax, visited the town. All the Big Four were ardent Republicans who had backed John C. Frémont in his bid for the presidency. Their control of the state's economy played a large part in making California a Republican stronghold from the end of the Civil War until after the Second World War.

The Nevada County Narrow Gauge Railroad had its eastern terminus at Colfax, where gold shipments from the mines of Grass Valley and Nevada City were loaded onto the main line. Built in 1874, the bed on which the ties were set was made of tailings from gold mines, leading some miners to prospect in the railbed. The railroad was very nearly abandoned in 1926, but the people of Nevada City and Grass Valley voted to continue its operation. The railroad finally met its demise in 1942, when its rails were used as scrap metal in the war effort. It must have been one of the richest short lines in history. Not only was its bed composed of gold mine tailings, it also carried bullion from the mines in excess of 300 million dollars.

In the spring of 1866, work began on Cape Horn, a granite promontory that blocked the forward progress of the railroad. Six thousand Chinese workmen, Crocker's pets, set to work at the task. Lowered from the top of the ledge in baskets, the Chinese first cut a narrow ledge with hammer and chisel. When this was completed, the ledge was widened with explosives and hand drills. Only twenty-eight miles of track were laid in 1866, at a total cost of $8,000,000, or about $285,000 for each mile. The summit tunnel, finished the following year, was the last major tunnel dug by hand.

The area around Colfax on the Divide is one of the most colorful in all the mining district. For some unknown reason, miners here exhausted their imaginations discovering new and hitherto unused names for creeks and hills. Nearby you will find Sucker Mountain rising above Shirttail Canyon. The canyon supposedly got its name when the miner who lived in it got too close to the fire in his nightshirt. The shirt caught fire and the miner ran out of the canyon to douse his shirttails in a nearby stream. The story was so amusing that the name was applied to the canyon and stuck there.

Dutch Flat   Dutch Flat, founded in 1851, was one of the largest mining towns in the 1850s, with 500 registered voters. Many important hydraulic mines were being worked in the vicinity. It was Dutch Flat to which Theodore Judah first turned for backing for his proposed transcontinental railroad, and here where he raised most of the money he needed. The merchants here stood to profit handsomely by selling their goods on the newly opened Comstock Lode, and to make certain that they did, they also organized the Dutch Flat and Donner Lake Wagon Road Company to improve the long-neglected road along this route.

Although it was the most direct route, the wagon route that led along the route of the Donner Party had never been improved to permit easy passage of freight wagons. In many places, like Cape Horn, large iron spikes were driven into sheer rock walls so that wagons could be lowered over them on ropes. This sort of maneuver was costly and time-consuming and prevented the road's wider use.

The Dutch Flat Wagon Road was a great success financially, for it permitted goods and building materials to be transported easily to advance construction sites on the route

of the railroad, as well as to Virginia City. Hostile newspaper editors charged that the owners of the Central Pacific
did not in fact intend to build a transcontinental railroad, but
instead only meant to build a short line to Dutch Flat, which
would permit them to monopolize trade with Nevada silver-
mining interests. They called the railroad the "Dutch Flat
Swindle" for five years until it became clear in 1866 that the
Central Pacific Railroad truly intended to cross the mountains after all.

Gold Run was another prosperous mining town until the *Gold Run*
Sawyer decision brought an end to hydraulic mining in 1882,
when its population dropped from 400 to 50 practically
overnight. Gold Run was located on the ridge route of the
Donner Pass emigrant trail, but another road ran to the
north through picturesque Bear Valley. This road rejoined
the main trail at Emigrant Gap. Since it has not yet been
developed, the Bear Valley trail offers an excellent opportunity to experience more vividly the passage of the early
emigrants. Rusty iron nails, horse shoes, and wagon irons
may sometimes be found on or near the trail.

North of Yuba Pass you will find the Grouse Lakes area. *Grouse Lakes*
No motorized vehicles are permitted in this part of the
forest, so that you may enjoy the alpine setting in its natural
condition. The restricted area comprises 18,000 acres, including all or parts of 120 lakes. The predominant vegetation
is composed of gnarled junipers, quaking aspen, and alpine
meadows. An added attraction is Meadow Lake, at the
eastern edge of the reserve and directly astride the Pacific
Crest trail.

During the summer of 1860 Henry Hartley came to
Meadow Lake to recover his health. After being cured of
tuberculosis, Hartley returned to the alpine setting in 1863
and discovered a ledge of gold-bearing quartz. The Union
Ledge was discovered the following year, but it was not until
1865 that the real boom started. In that year 3,000 souls,
responding to newspaper articles that proclaimed this "a
second Comstock," founded Summit City. Astonishingly, *Summit City*
no assays were run on the ore samples that were the foundation of this boom.

Though winter storms drove most residents to the safety
of lower elevations, the following spring saw a renewal of

interest. Companies were formed, stocks sold, shafts sunk, and mills constructed. Four hundred buildings were built and seventy-two stamps were ready to begin pulverizing ore. The bubble burst when the first ore samples assayed at only three dollars to the ton. Altogether, two million dollars had been expended with no hope of any return.

The city was soon abandoned save for a few stalwarts hoping to find a new ledge, and in 1873 fire destroyed most of the remaining buildings. A brief flurry of excitement was aroused in 1875 when a new process for extracting the gold was announced, but it too proved worthless.

In a sense, the story of Summit City is the story of the gold rush in microcosm. The new claim was made and many profited handsomely from the discovery. A small amount of gold was extracted (in this case, a very small amount), and the gold field subsequently abandoned. With the exception of a few large towns, this is what happened all over the golden hills. There were literally hundreds of such towns, all of them now vanished save for a few stone houses or foundations and perhaps a cemetery.

The original route of the pioneers over Donner Summit was south of the present one. It was at Donner Lake in 1846 that the most famous of all pioneer tragedies occurred. Here a party of emigrants was forced to spend the winter with hardly any food or fuel while their huts were buried by snowdrifts.

Donner Party

The Donner Party, led by George and Jacob Donner and James F. Reed, had set out for California in the spring of 1846 with a party of Illinois farmers. Instead of following the regular route to the coast, the Donner Party decided to take the Hastings cut-off, which they supposed to be a shorter and easier route. The contrary proved to be the case, however, and they found themselves passing through deserts and over mountain ranges that were far more difficult to cross than those on the more customary route, leading as it did across the alkaline deserts of Utah and Nevada. Having lost much precious time on this shortcut, the Donner Party nevertheless elected to cross the Sierra Nevada at the end of October.

Even though the winter snows had begun falling, the party of men, women, and children still might have been

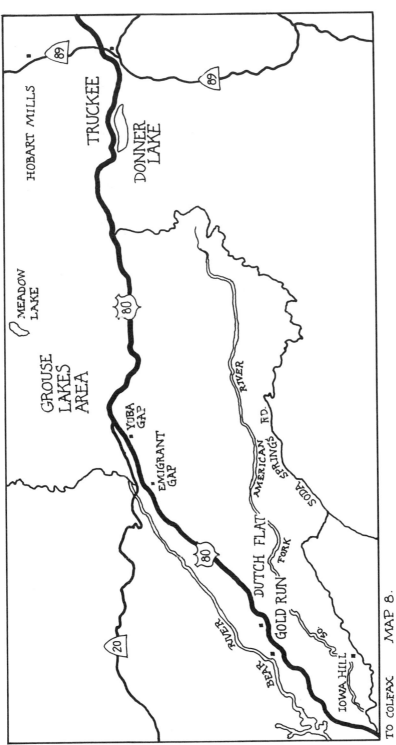

TO COLFAX   MAP 8.

able to cross the summit were it not for the delay of a single day. Having found the pass and made all preparations to cross, the party went to sleep with the intention of setting out early the next morning. But a new snowfall obliterated the trail during the night, and it was determined that the group should await a break in the weather before attempting a crossing.

The break never came. Moreover, through panic and carelessness, most of the oxen, which might have provided food during the long winter ahead, were lost in the snow. As the winter progressed and game grew scarce at this elevation, the emigrants at length realized their plight.

Curiously, a lone emigrant named Moses Schallenberger had spent the previous winter at the same spot where the Donners now found themselves. He had never come close to starvation, but had survived by trapping foxes and eating their meat. He also found coyotes in his traps, but he pronounced them inedible after many attempts at different methods of preparing their meat.

Whether the Donner Party were too numerous to survive in this manner, or whether they simply panicked when faced with the ordeal, it is impossible to say. Certainly, the older members of the party and the children soon began to sicken and die on the meager diet they could manage. At last, the desperate pioneers sent a "forlorn hope" party on ahead in the hope that they might reach the Central Valley and bring back help before the entire wagon train had perished. Setting out in the middle of December, this group included ten young men and women, the strongest from the larger party. Only three women and two men survived the thirty-two-day crossing, but on their arrival in California a group of expert mountaineers was dispatched to rescue those left behind.

The relief party reached the cabins by Donner Lake on February 18. There they found the starved remnants of the original wagon train, which had included some eighty souls. Although the rescue party attempted to lead most of those who had been stranded to safety, they could not save everyone: of the eighty who reached Donner Lake in October, only forty survived the ordeal.

The worst was yet to come. Those who were reluctant or

unable to make the trek out with the first relief party suffered further privations until, maddened by hunger, cold and isolation, they lost the last thin veneer of civilization and reverted to primitive savagery. Several resorted to cannibalizing their dead companions in their struggle to survive. At least one became a thief, attempting to steal the money George Donner had collected from the rest for safekeeping. More than one may have committed murder on their weaker fellows. Incidentally, this episode of murder, theft, and cannibalism occurred, not on Donner Lake, but several miles down the trail, on Alder Creek.

The gruesome events of the past contrast markedly with the beauty of the setting. In winter, the snows which sealed the fate of the Donner Party have become the playground of skiing enthusiasts from all over the world. There are several famous ski resorts within a few minutes' drive of the lake.

Truckee

The mountain resort town of Truckee lies not far from Donner Lake. Ironically, this town takes its name from the Indian guide, Truckee, who had guided the Stevens-Townsend-Murphy party safely over the pass the previous winter. The first wagon train to cross the mountains, the Stevens party, had left young Schallenberger behind at the lake to guard their property. Truckee himself discovered Mountain Lake, which bore the name Truckee Lake until the Donner Party gave it their own name by their sufferings. The town was known as Coburn's Station until 1864 and was a regular stop on the way to the Washoe silver-mining districts. The Indian Truckee later became a member of Frémont's battalion and died in 1860.

Hobart Mills

The road north (Highway 89) from Truckee leads to Hobart Mills, named for the lumber mill constructed there in 1896. Employing 500 men, the lumber mill turned out 175,000 board feet per shift. Beyond Hobart Mills the road leads to Sierra County.

Lake Tahoe

Interstate 80 follows the course of the Truckee River down to Reno, while two other highways lead south toward Lake Tahoe. Unquestionably the jewel of the Sierra Nevada,

Twain on Tahoe

At last the Lake burst upon us—a noble sheet of blue water lifted six thousand three hundred feet above the level of the sea, and walled in by a rim of snow-clad mountain peaks that towered aloft full three thousand feet higher still! It was a vast oval, and one would have to use up eighty or a hundred good miles in traveling around it. As it lay there with the shadows of the mountains brilliantly photographed upon its still surface I thought it must surely be the fairest picture the whole earth affords. It was a delicious solitude we were in, too. Three miles away was a saw-mill and some workmen, but there were not fifteen other human beings throughout the wide circumference of the lake. As the darkness closed down and the stars came out and spangled the great mirror with jewels, we smoked meditatively in the solemn hush and forgot our troubles and our pains. In due time we spread our blankets in the warm sand between two boulders and soon fell asleep, . . . lulled to sleep by the beating of the surf upon the shore . . . I think that hardly any amount of fatigue can be gathered together that a man cannot sleep off in one night by its side.

So singularly clear was the water, that where it was only twenty or thirty feet deep the bottom was so perfectly distince that the boat seemed floating in the air! Yes, where it was even *eighty* feet deep. Every little pebble was distinct, every speckled trout, every hand's-breadth of sand. . . . Down through the transparency of these great depths, the water was not *merely* transparent, but dazzingly, brilliantly so.

Mark Twain, *Roughing It*

Boating on Donner Lake (*Nordhoff's* California)

Tahoe is the largest lake in the range. Formerly remarkable for its crystal clarity, the water of the lake has suffered some pollution in recent years from the proliferation of houses and resorts on its shores.

Tahoe was not discovered by the earlier explorers like Joseph Walker and Jedediah Smith, whose passage through the mountains led them further south. Instead, the honor for its discovery went to John C. Frémont. Frémont was leading an expedition in search of a large body of water, named Mary's Lake, and the Buenaventura River, which was supposed to flow into the Pacific through a gap in the mountains. When neither of the two could be found, Frémont headed into California against the orders of his commanding officers. On his way across the Sierra, in February, 1844, Frémont and his party sighted the lake in the distance. He named it Lake Bonpland after the botanist who had accompanied Baron von Humboldt on the latter's epoch-making voyage of discovery to South and Central America.

The lake was renamed Bigler in 1852, after the governor of California, but the name was changed in 1863 when Tahoe City was first laid out—at the same time that gold was being dug out of Squaw Valley. The Civil War was raging in the East, and the Reverend F. Starr King suggested that Bigler, who was a secessionist, should not have so noble a body of water named for him. Starr King had come to the West expressly to rally support for the Union cause; instead of Bigler, he suggested the name Tahoe, which means "Big Water" in the Washoe dialect.

Among other visitors to the lake was Mark Twain, who gave a lengthy account of his adventures on its shores in his account of his western travels, *Roughing It*. Lake Tahoe remains clear, though not so clear as Twain described it. Some parts of its shoreline remain isolated and undeveloped, but new and thriving communities have grown up beside its waters. As time goes on, will this once miraculously clear lake become just another of the world's wonders that have been spoiled by too many people visiting them? Or will we find a way to assure that civilization does not destroy the works of nature, so that our grandchildren and great-grandchildren will still be able to marvel as did Mark Twain that "so empty and airy did all spaces seem below us, and so strong was the sense of floating high aloft in mid-nothingness, that we called these boat-excursions 'balloon-voyages.'"

Part Three:

Nevada County and the Gold-Mining Industry

Nevada County had a great deal to do with making America what it is today. In 1848, when gold was discovered, the country was young and predominantly rural. The vast network of railroads that was to link East with West was only a dream. Engineers were a rare breed; inventors were far more likely to live in Europe. Life was simple, and a man did not need much education to cope with his needs.

More than any other single fact, the discovery of gold changed all that. Gold was the catalyst that developed the West, that pushed through the railroads and the telegraph lines—it should come as no surprise that the first long-distance telephone hook-up in the country was here in Nevada County.

Elsewhere, progress was slow, hardly even noticeable. We are all familiar with the peaceful existence Mark Twain describes in the Midwest of his boyhood. When Twain describes the West after the Gold Rush, we enter a different world. The men are workers, working at industrial jobs around the clock. The pace is hectic. Men become millionaires overnight and paupers just as soon again. Speculation in stocks runs rampant, and everywhere are machines: steam drills for the mines; hoists and elevators; stamping machines to crush the ore; and railroads to carry the ore to the cities.

In Grass Valley, Nevada City, and at the Malakoff Diggings (north on Highway 49 from Auburn or Highway 174 from Colfax), you will learn a lot about the nature of our society, how it got the way it is and where it may be headed.

Grass Valley

Grass Valley has always been one of the most attractive towns in California. Nestled in a valley that seems to protect it from the outside world, this old mining center was built on a small, human scale. Even during its heyday, when hundreds of stamps were running in the neighborhood, at the Empire and the North Star mines, visitors to Grass Valley could hardly believe that they were actually in a *mining* town— mining towns were supposed to be dirty, with a cloud of smoke hanging perpetually in the air, and noisy, with the continual drone of stamps rising and falling, monotonously, day and night. But here was a small, peaceful town, with clean air and quiet breezes and hardly a hint that men were working deep underground extracting precious metal from tunnels blasted through the earth.

There were many reasons for this. In the first place, there was the Pelton wheel. Power to run the mines was provided by water, quietly and cleanly. The mines were located to the south of the town, just far enough away that they did not interfere with the normal day-to-day business of the town. Small wonder that Lola Montez, who had seen much of the world, decided to build her home here.

Maidu The inhabitants of the region when white men first arrived were the Maidu peoples, who fished for salmon in the waters of Wolf Creek during the annual spring run. White men first arrived here soon after the discovery of gold at Coloma, and the first cabins began appearing on Badger Hill and in nearby Boston Ravine, where the North Star Mining Museum now stands.

Relations between the natives and the newcomers were at first amicable, but that soon changed. Samuel Holt and James Walsh began constructing a sawmill on Wolf Creek in Boston Ravine during November. The small party was attacked by Indians the following May, probably because the

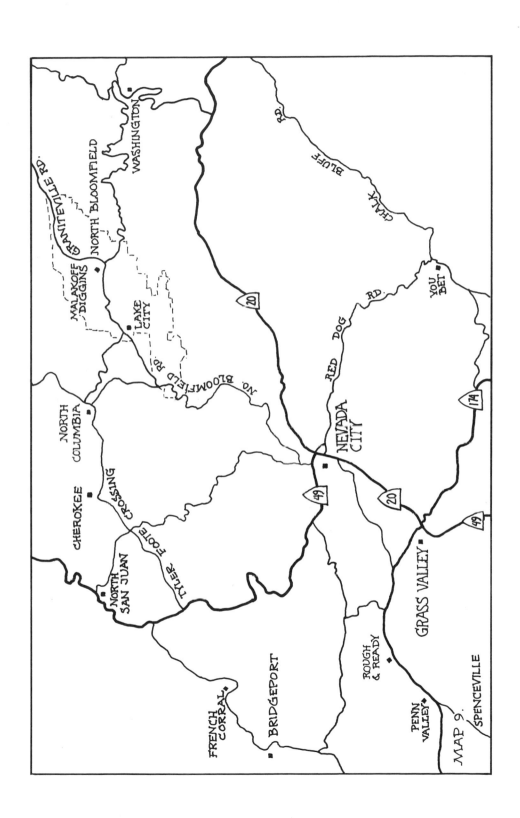

MAP 9.

mill dam was interfering with the salmon run. The Indians killed one man and let the other five go, although they destroyed the offending sawmill. Amid exaggerated reports of 700 bloodthirsty savages, the U.S. Army sent twenty-four soldiers, who, together with a vigilante group of 100 miners, killed or drove off all the Indians in the region.

Gold Hill

The placer deposits here were not very rich, but quartz gold was discovered in an outcropping on Gold Hill by George Knight in October, 1850. If ever there was a "tip of the iceberg" that concealed far more than it revealed, this little outcropping was it: Over the next 108 years, more than $130 million in gold was taken from Gold Hill, most of it from the North Star and Empire mines, making this the richest deposit in the state and one of the richest anywhere in the world. The site of this discovery is marked by a plaque near Boston Ravine on Cornwall Street.

The year 1851 was a time of rapid growth for Grass Valley, thanks to the newly discovered gold deposits. The houses were wooden and did not survive the fire of 1855. Besides quartz mining, there were flourishing lumber mills and a number of hotels. But Grass Valley is perhaps best known for the many celebrated people who lived here at one time or another during the 1850s. One who exerted a lasting influence over life in California was Isaac Owen, a Methodist minister who preached the first sermon in Grass Valley in the shade of an oak. Owen moved on—Californians always seemed afflicted by restlessness—to Santa Clara on the shores of San Francisco Bay, where he founded the College of the Pacific and transformed that tiny town into the intellectual center of the state.

Lola Montez

The most notorious resident of this gold-mining camp was Lola Montez, a truly remarkable woman. After eloping with a gallant young soldier when she was but nineteen years old, Lola soon found herself alone in the world. Although she was Irish by birth, Lola used her dark eyes and hair to good advantage as a Spanish dancer, first in London and later on the continent. Her dancing never received great accolades— her most famous routine involved rubber spiders, hidden in the folds of her costume, which fell to the stage as they were shaken loose by the movements of her dance—but Lola had great charm and wit. She soon captivated the artistic world

Lola Montez *(Courtesy, The Bancroft Library)*

of Europe. Franz Liszt, George Sand, and Frederic Chopin were numbered among her acquaintances. Her most important conquest was King Ludwig of Bavaria. As his mistress, Lola dictated the tastes of his court and patronized the arts. Her efforts nearly led to the overthrow of the king in 1848, however, and Lola was forced to flee by angry mobs. She did obtain the title of Countess of Lansfeld for her troubles, but the title had no income attached to it, so Lola returned to the stage and made her spiders start earning their keep.

The call of California drew the Countess to San Francisco in 1851, where she was welcomed with open arms. The spiders, however, did not appeal to local audiences, so Lola arranged a tour of the goldfields. The miners were even less gracious than the San Franciscans had been. At one performance she was openly jeered and refused to continue her act. The tour dissolved and Lola decided to retire to Grass

Valley, where she built a house at the corner of Mill and Walsh streets. Her retirement was short-lived, for Lola returned to the stage, first as a dancer in Australia, then as a lecturer in America. She died in New York in 1861 at the age of forty-two.

Lotta Crabtree

Lola Montez lived long enough in Grass Valley to scandalize the local matrons and to encourage the career of a young dancer, Lotta Crabtree. Lotta's mother ran a boarding house on Mill Street before putting her daughter on the stage. Tiny and full of energy, Lotta soon became the darling of the miners. Perhaps most of all, Lotta reminded the miners of home in the East, of wives and sweethearts they had left behind as they sought their fortune, and of children whose absence in the rough mining towns was keenly felt. Lotta retired while still young with a large fortune. She never married, but lived alone until her death in 1924 at age seventy-seven, and left a fortune in excess of $4,000,000 to charity.

Amos Delano

A name which was well known in the early days of the state but which has been forgotten by posterity is that of Amos Delano, express agent, humorist, and possessor of the largest nose in California. Born in 1806, Delano came west with the rest of the gold seekers. He earned local renown in Grass Valley on two occasions during the 1850s. Once, when a fire had destroyed much of the business district, including the Wells Fargo office, Delano salvaged the safe and pushed a shack up against it in order to keep his doors open for business. On another occasion, when Wells Fargo suffered financial setbacks and ordered its agents to stop making payments, Delano ignored the instruction and promised to make good on all accounts from his own pocket if necessary.

To the reading public, Delano was better known as Old Block, and his items appeared regularly in newspapers all over the state, together with caricatures he had drawn. Once he explained the derivation of his name in the following manner:

> Old Block . . . came very near being descended from a high family, his great ancestor being compelled to fly from France in Huguenot times, to save his neck from the gallows, and keep his feet on the ground. His

mother either was or had a head; at all events, she had some go-ahead about her, so that being Head, on one side, and Block, on the other, he claims a lineal descent from the great family of Blockheads, so numerous in our community, and inherits, in a remarkable degree, the peculiarities of that remarkable family.

Delano published *Pen Knife Sketches* and *Life on the Plains and among the Diggings*, both humorous accounts of life in gold rush California. He died in 1878.

A man who exerted more influence in his day than any of the above residents of Grass Valley was born in 1855 in a house where the library stands today. He was Josiah Royce, who spent his first eleven years in this town before leaving for San Francisco and, later, Harvard University. His mother, Sarah Eleanor Royce, organized the first school in Grass Valley and encouraged her son's intellectual pursuits. Josiah went to Harvard to study philosophy with William James and remained as James's disciple and successor. He became the foremost philosopher of his day, writing prolifically on every subject under the sun, including a book on California history.

Josiah Royce

Royce considered himself a born nonconformist and attributed this trait to his California heritage. In an early essay, he epitomized that heritage as one that taught him to think "independently, because I am a Californian, as little bound to follow mere tradition as I am liable to find an audience by preaching in this wilderness; reverently, because I am thinking and writing face to face with a mighty and lovely Nature, by the side of whose greatness I am but a worm."

Are not these the characteristics shared by all of these early Californians? And cannot nonconformity and reverence for nature be used to describe Californians of today?

Despite its intellectual and artistic beginnings, Grass Valley soon became better known for its mining activities. The intricacies of quartz mining were not well understood when gold was first discovered embedded in a quartz outcropping in 1850. The gold-bearing vein, or ledge, was believed to be continuous and to extend beneath the ground indefinitely. Consequently, a large number of ambitious miners took out claims on sections of the ledge in much the same way that they took out claims on sections of gold-bearing sand. As it turned out, the development of quartz mines required larger investments of time and money than these early miners had anticipated, and many of them went bankrupt within the first few years.

After the first boom times, Grass Valley suffered a depression. Many miners left, and the stores and hotels that had been built to accommodate them either closed down or went on operating at a loss. Then came a second boom, as new technologies were developed and new mines were formed by consolidating smaller outfits and operating them more economically on a larger scale. In 1867, the mines in Grass Valley were operating collectively 248 stamps. These stamps crushed over 70,000 tons of ore with an average yield of from thirty to thirty-five dollars per ton. Production in 1869 amounted to nearly $1,700,000 of gold.

Demand for gold was high during the Civil War (1860–1865), since the Union required gold to pay its bills to European suppliers. Spurred on by government demand, mine operators kept on expanding their operations even when they were losing money by doing so. The Idaho mine encountered ore at 300 feet in 1867 and produced nearly $12,000,000 in the next twenty-seven years.

The other mines were not so fortunate. Panic spread through the Eastern financial centers in 1873 and dried up any further funds for investment. The North Star mine closed down in 1874 and the Eureka followed suit in 1877. Only the Empire kept its head above water. Its owner, W. B. Bourne, Jr., was advised to close down in 1878 by three mining experts but elected to keep going anyway. It was a wise decision. The depression was bottoming out in the East and money soon became available for further development. Bourne's gamble paid off by making him the owner of the North Star as well—he purchased it in 1884. During the next decade, the North Star alone produced $2,500,000 worth of gold.

Modern Grass Valley is a pleasant community with much to attract the tourist. Although it has endured rapid growth in recent years, the town retains a small town atmosphere and has kept much of its downtown area intact. There are numerous small shops which make walking around a delight, while many small but fascinating Victorian houses line the lanes leading out of the downtown area.

The Lola Montez house is now the headquarters for the Nevada County Arts Council, on Mill Street. Nearby are Lotta Crabtree's residence and a plaque in front of the library to mark Josiah Royce's birthplace. Also on Mill Street is a small bakery selling Cornish pasties, a meat pie that the miners could hold in one hand. The hardrock miners of Cornwall, in England, formed the backbone of the community during the latter half of the nineteenth century. Many English traditions have been transplanted to this region, of which the best known is the Tommyknocker. He is the ghost of a miner who was killed in a cave-in. Naturally, given the cause of his demise, the Tommyknocker is fearful of the imminent collapse of any building he finds himself in; consequently, he can be heard knocking the timbers of houses to make sure they are sound.

The most distinctive structure on Main Street is the Holbrooke Hotel, dating from the 1850s. It is a charming building with a long history and still functions as a hotel and restaurant.

Holbrooke Hotel

Grass Valley Mining Museum: An excellent example of what can be done for a small, local museum, using love and hard work with very little money, can be found at the foot of Mill Street in Boston Ravine. The museum is housed in the recently restored powerhouse of the North Star Mine. This building provided the power used to drive pumps and machinery at the North Star Mine, not far to the south.

Inside the museum, the most important display is the thirty-foot Pelton wheel, the largest of its kind in the world. The Pelton wheel is a kind of water wheel, patented by Lester Pelton in 1880. Pelton, then a resident of Camptonville, invented the wheel as a means of harnessing the energy of the mountain streams which were so abundant, in order to replace the burning of wood to fuel steam engines when the nearby forests had been denuded. The timing of the invention was critical: It coincided with the demise of hydraulic mining, when vast quantities of water suddenly became available for uses besides washing away gold-bearing gravel. Hundreds of miles of aqueducts and dozens of dams had been

Pelton Wheel

constructed at great cost for gigantic mining operations which were now illegal. The waters impounded in these dams were used to supply power for air compressors that operated other mine equipment. Within a few years, advancements on the Pelton wheel made possible the conversion of water into electricity, and California became one of the world's leading centers of electrical research and hydroelectric construction.

The Pelton wheel housed here was the forerunner of all these later developments. When in operation, this wheel turned sixty-five times a minute and generated 1,000 horsepower. The rim of the wheel attained a speed of seventy-five miles per hour. The Pelton wheel was originally enclosed so that nothing was visible while it was turning—this was to prevent water from spraying all over the place.

Other exhibits inside the museum stress the technological developments made during the history of lode mining and techniques developed to process the gold ore once it was brought to the surface. The mines in this area were started with sledge hammers and hand-held jack drills. Rock was blasted loose by inserting black powder into the holes; then it was carried away with pick and shovel. The mining carts were sometimes pulled by mules that never left the mine tunnels once they were lowered down the shaft in a special sling.

Among the developments that assisted the miners and greatly increased productivity were the high-compression Leyner drills, similar to the modern jack-hammer, and dynamite, also called "giant powder," which was hard to use and caused a few accidents before miners managed to control its destructive force.

The apparatus used in refining the ore is also on display here. There are stamps and shaker tables used in the amalgamation process—the process whereby gold was mixed with mercury in order to remove it from the baser metals also present in the ore. Amalgamation depends on the similarity between mercury and gold (they are adjacent elements on the periodic chart), which causes them to form a loose bond. The resultant mixture, or amalgam, was then separated from the rest of the ore and heated to 500 degrees Fahrenheit, at which point the mercury vaporized and gold remained.

Hardrock Mining (*Courtesy, The Bancroft Library*)

The mercury could be used over and over. The gold was then further refined to remove all impurities before it was poured into molds.

Outside the museum are several large pieces of equipment including a man skip, which was used to transport men down into the mine, and a Cornish pump, which was used to pump water out of the mines. Naturally, keeping a hole thousands of feet deep free of water was a difficult task.

The grounds of the North Star Mine, which lie to the south of the museum, have fallen victim to urbanization and been subdivided into condominiums.

Empire Mine State Historic Park: The grounds of the Empire Mine have been rescued from developers by the State Park system, which is in the process of making a large and fascinating historical exhibit on the site. Unfortunately, the process has been slow, but the park is well worth a visit, even in its present condition. The massive groundworks are reminiscent of the Palatine Hill in Rome, where the Caesars built their palaces and ruled the ancient world. Here, a different kind of monarch ruled: His name was William Bourne, Jr., and he maintained a residence on the grounds. Bourne and his family lived in baronial splendor in the Empire Cottage, surrounded by its lawns, gardens and ponds. This was only one of his four houses, a remarkable conception built of rough-hewn stone in 1898, when Bourne was at the height of his wealth and power. It is open to guided tours.

Many of the Empire's buildings have been demolished, and much of its equipment was sold to other operations when the mine was closed in 1956, but an impressive assortment of compressors, winches, pumps and generators can be seen in the open yard on the other side of the stone fence around the parking lot. This equipment provides a vivid historical record of the progress in the mine from steam power, to water (with the aid of the Pelton wheel), and finally to electrical power. The machine shop is large and filled with primitive power tools, all of them powered by a complex network of overhead gears and canvas bands.

The headframe of the Empire was located near the carpentry shop. The ninety-four-foot-high structure was used to lift ore and waste rock out of the mine and lower men into it. You can still see the opening of the mine, but only with the aid of a vivid imagination can you envision what lies beneath the ground. Mere numbers can only help a little: The main shaft extends straight down the incline for 4,600 feet. It connects with 367 miles of tunnels, the deepest of which comes to an end 11,007 feet away and 6,000 feet below the surface of the ground. It took a man nearly eight minutes to ride the skip from the bottom of the shaft to daylight at a speed of 800 feet per minute. Men traveled only half as fast as ore skips, for safety reasons, but accidents still happened when an arm or a leg was left carelessly hanging outside the open skip, or a skip was sent to the wrong level by mistake.

The stamp mill was located to the west of the carpentry shop. Only the foundations remain. At one time the building housed eighty stamps, each weighing 1,750 pounds.

To the southwest of the stamp mill was the cyanide plant, constructed in 1905 to take advantage of a new process for refining gold from ore. In this process, the ore was washed with sodium cyanide, which carried off the gold and deposit-

"The Hungry Convention"

A curiously burlesque assembly gathered together in Grass Valley in the winter of 1852–3, and is known in local history as "the Hungry Convention." The winter had been so severe that supplies were short: bacon and flour had once again risen to the prices of 1849. Miners could not work their claims, and were assembled in the town, spoiling for some enterprise or excitement. So a meeting was called, in dignified earnest, to consider whether the scarcity of provisions could in any manner be relieved. Everyone soon saw that, in the condition of the roads, there was nothing for it except patience: the merchants would secure supplies at the earliest moment possible. The meeting immediately degenerated into a wild burlesque. Speeches of the most desperate and communistic order were made, and hailed with shouts of laughter and applause. A duly elected committee reported, declaring war upon San Francisco, and their resolve to have supplies thence "peacably if we can, forcibly if we must."

Charles Howard Shinn, *Mining Camps*, 1885

ed it on zinc plates. This process increased productivity at the Empire mine by 40 percent. Elsewhere, the cyanide process made the industry of gold dredging possible, since old tailings piles could be treated and more gold could be recovered from them. The cyanide plant is also a ruin.

Hardrock Trail: The cyanide plant marks the beginning of the hardrock trail, a two-and-one-half mile loop that takes two hours to complete. Among other historic sites along this trail are the Cassidy, Pennsylvania, and W.Y.O.D. (Work Your Own Diggins) mines. The name of W.Y.O.D. was somewhat paradoxical, since it was discovered that its ore-body was an extension of the Pennsylvania mine's

In and About Nevada City

Nevada City, it should be borne in mind, is not a town in the state of Nevada, but is in California among the Sierra Nevada mountains, on the western slope, situated on Deer creek, eight miles south of the south fork of the Yuba river, and about four miles northeast of Grass valley, so called by those who first came to Nevada City taking their cattle there to pasture, there being no grass near the town. Gold had not yet been discovered in Grass valley. About half way between the two places was what was afterwards called Gold Run, that eventually proved to be very rich, and which I shall have occasion to allude to hereafter. Down Deer creek about four miles was Boyer's Agency. He was supposed to be some kind of an Indian agent, although I was never able to learn what he did for the Indians or any one else but himself. This remark is not intended in disparagement of Mr. Boyer, but only that I can't see what the government or the Indians wanted of an agent there. About half way between Boyer's and Nevada City was Wood's Ravine, so named after a man of that name who lived there and afterwards officiated as alcada or magistrate. About nine miles down Deer creek was Rough and Ready diggings, named, I suppose, from the political campaign title bestowed on President Taylor; but this place was even less complimentary to the President than was suggested by the name, for a harder and more dismal place I never saw.

Nevada City was laid out in a deep ravine. It had its Main street and its Broad street and its Kiota street parallel with Main and a few cross streets. What buildings were erected in my time were on Main and Broad principally.

Charles D. Ferguson, *California Gold Fields*, 1888

ledge—in other words, all the ore in the W.Y.O.D. actually belonged to the Pennsylvania. Sights along the way include old tailings piles and the foundations of several structures connected with the operations of the Empire and its associated mines.

Be sure to see the headframe of the Rowe mine, across the street from the parking lot, on your way out. This structure, seventy-five feet high, was known as a gallows in some quarters because of its resemblance to the platform used in formal hangings.

At the other end of town from the Empire mine is a monument to the man who may have been the first to fly in a heavier-than-air craft. Located at the west end of Main Street is the site of Lyman Gilmore's air field, the first commercial air field in the United States. Lyman Gilmore was an early aviator and longtime resident of Grass Valley. According to a document whose veracity can neither be proven nor disproven, Gilmore successfully flew a glider equipped with a twenty-horsepower steam engine on or before May 15, 1902—more than eighteen months before the Wright brothers made their famous flight at Kitty Hawk. Whether or not this was true, Gilmore was certainly an important pioneer in aviation history. Today the site of the air field is occupied by a school named after the inventor.

Lyman Gilmore

Nevada City

Nevada City is the county seat of Nevada County, located only a few minutes' drive north of Grass Valley. The town was founded before Grass Valley, the first cabin having been put up in September, 1849, when the place was known as Deer Creek Dry Diggins. James Marshall actually paid a visit to Deer Creek in 1848, after his discovery at Coloma, but he did not find gold here.

The first store was started in October, 1849, by Dr. A. B. Caldwell and some friends. After that, the place was referred to as Caldwell's Upper Store, until it was officially named Nevada City in the following year.

That year marked an incredible boom for Nevada City, as the rich placer deposits began to attract miners from all over the state. Twelve thousand men were at work in its gullies and washes by the end of 1850. Quartz mining caused another boom, or rather a continuation of the first, so that by 1856, Nevada City polled the third highest number of voters in the state. Between 15,000 and 35,000 miners were digging within a seven-mile circuit of the town, which could boast 150 stores, 14 hotels, and 400 houses.

Coyoteville

Among the richest of the suburbs, and surely the most famous, was Coyoteville, also known as Coyote Hill. The camp was located at one end of the Coyote Lead, a placer deposit that was one mile long and 100 yards wide. First struck in May of 1850, the Coyote Lead yielded $8,000,000 of gold by 1856. The lead and the camp took their name from the method used to extract the gold-bearing gravel, which required men to dig trenches like the burrows of coyotes. At the bottom of the hill these trenches were only six to eight feet deep, but the lead got deeper and deeper so that the trenches further up the hill might be as much as 100 feet deep. The ditch from Mosquito Creek, which brought water to the miners for their long toms, was reputedly the first ditch in the state in March of 1850. A Frenchman named Chabot used a hose to wash the dirt from his claim in 1852, while Edward E. Mattesen invented hydraulic mining on American Hill in the following year.

Actually, Mattesen only rediscovered a process known to the ancient Romans and described by the ancient author Pliny in his work on natural history. The Romans used a form of hydraulicking that was known to the California miners as booming. They released the whole contents of a reservoir onto a mass of gold-bearing dirt and gravel which had been undermined by pick and shovel. The water then carried the dirt away by means of a sluice that was dug in the ground and lined with stones to capture the heavier particles of gold.

Today Coyoteville is noteworthy for the three- and four-story houses that cling precariously to its canyon walls. These houses can be seen on the way out of town to the north. The former camp of Coyoteville now forms the northwest corner of Nevada City.

Nevada City itself has many picturesque and historic

Nevada City, c. 1852 *(California State Library)*

buildings. The "Washington Monument Church," originally Congregational but now Baptist, rivals Grass Valley's
religious and educational claims, for it was on this site in
1853 that a joint session of the Congregational Association of
California and the Presbytery of San Francisco met to discuss
the establishment of an institution of higher learning in the
state. Professor Henry Durant attended the meeting and
took part in the discussions, which led to the founding of the
College of California, later to become the University of
California. The present church was built in 1864 after fire
had destroyed two previous structures on the site.

The courthouse also replaces two previous structures. It is
an intriguing design strongly influenced by the Art Deco
styles of the 1930s. Nevada City's position as county seat
made its residents preeminent in the field of law and government. Among the early lawyers practicing here was William

William M.
Stewart

M. Stewart, a specialist in mining claims and related litigation who rose to eminence in Virginia City.

Stewart was one of the most colorful and influential characters in the history of the West. As a law student at Yale in 1849 he heard the siren call of gold and left college on a Panama-bound steamer. Stewart struck it rich at Buckeye Hill (part of Coyoteville) and took his money into the legal profession with him. He finished his studies with a local attorney—lawyers were scarce and colleges nonexistent—and served as local district attorney for two years. Stewart remained in Nevada City until 1860, when he departed for the Comstock Lode. The fortune he made in silver at Virginia City was lost in silver at Panamint Valley, but Stewart managed to get himself elected senator from Nevada in the meantime. The crusty old 49er was working on amassing another fortune when he died in 1909.

Aaron Sargent

Another district attorney was Aaron Augustus Sargent, who also started the first newspaper published in the goldfields, the *Nevada Journal*, in 1852. Sargent helped found the Republican Party in California and attended the convention that nominated Abraham Lincoln for president in 1860. Sargent himself served in the U.S. House of Representatives and in the Senate before President Grant appointed him ambassador to Germany. Like the true Californian he was, Sargent proved too outspoken for the diplomatic service. He called Otto von Bismarck a liar and was hastily recalled. Among his other accomplishments was a history of the early days in Nevada County.

Lorenzo Sawyer

The third lawyer who made his start in the old courthouse was Lorenzo Sawyer, the judge who was involved in the first major environmental lawsuit in the state. Sawyer's early days in California were spent in fruitless pursuit of legal cases, both in San Francisco and here. His first big break came in a murder case that none of the other lawyers would handle.

The defendant was known as "Old Harriet," and she ran a brothel on the banks of Deer Creek. One day the body of an old miner, who had last been seen at Harriet's place with a large poke, was found in a whirlpool downstream from the scene of his nighttime antics. As the body was naked, things

---

Gold and Quartz

Wherever gold is discovered in California, particles of quartz are found adhering to it more or less; this quartz, even when found at great depths, is generally rounded by the action of water, for quartz, when detached by violent action, is naturally angular, and inclined to splinter, and from its hardness it must require ages to give it the form of a pebble, by the slow process of grinding it receives in a comparatively dry mountain gorge. This, taken in conjunction with the facts that the gold is found now on the surface, and now low down resting on the bed rock, here forced into clefts of granite, and again in clusters of small pear-shaped nuggets, as if the metal had been ejected by intense heat, and had dripped from the volcanic boulders that lie scattered around; tends to bear out the supposition that disintegrated gold has been cast into places that time and accident alone can reveal, and that the original opinion that the gold was on the surface only no longer holds good.

Frank Marryat, *Mountains and Molehills*, 1855

---

looked black for Old Harriet, and when a second body was discovered a few days later, at the same place and in the same condition, the townsfolk began to think about a hanging. However, Sawyer explained the two bodies very simply: The two met on the bridge above the whirlpool, got into a quarrel over the money, fell into the river and drowned, the action of the turbulent waters stripping the clothes from their bodies. The money, in the form of gold dust, was washed away. The jury acquitted the innocent madam, and Sawyer's ingenuity made him the most sought-after lawyer in the county. Sawyer later rose to become district judge, chief justice of the Supreme Court, and finally was appointed to the federal bench by President Grant.

Just as important to the life of the community as the court-house was the Miner's Foundry, now a part of the American Victorian Museum, at the corner of Spring and Bridge streets. Here were cast the essential equipment for mining, the ore buckets, skips, and other pieces of equipment. The foundry also made the wheels for the first street railway to connect Grass Valley and Nevada City, built in 1901 and discontinued in 1926 in the middle of a snowstorm.

The Victorian Museum also includes a house furnished in the style of the period, a theater, a restaurant, and a radio station. Currently, the museum is trying to raise money in order to install the Tremont Facade, a wood and plaster building front that once graced the Tremont Hotel in Red Bluff, California.

The movie theater on Broad Street stands on an historic site. The first theater, the Cedar, was built here during the hectic days of the gold rush. Some of the finest entertainers in the world appeared on its boards, as a regular theater circuit was quickly established to serve the bored (but well-heeled) miners. Most of the early entertainers have been forgotten, but one name stands out after all these years: Edwin Booth, the brother of Lincoln's assassin and a fine Shakespearean actor. Booth performed here and throughout the golden hills. The miners, mostly scions of middle-class families in the East and well-educated as a rule, knew their Shakespeare. Careless thespians who flubbed a line frequently had the correct one shouted back at them from the audience. Good performers were regarded with showers of gold nuggets, while shoddy acts were driven from the stage with hoots of derision.

The original theater burned in 1858 and was not replaced until after the Civil War, when the Nevada Theater was built. Construction had to be halted on March 26, 1865, when news of President Lincoln's assassination reached the town and a period of general mourning ensued.

The Nevada Theater had some well-known performers of its own. Mark Twain gave a lecture there during the first tour that launched his career. Emma Nevada, a world-renowned opera star who was born in nearby Alpha in 1862, gave a special performance here in 1891. Her first appearance had been at the Nevada City Baptist Church, after which she had gone on to sing in Vienna and other European capitals. Her voice was touching in the particular sentimental style that thrilled our Victorian ancestors; her closing number was always "The Last Rose of Summer," a heart-wrenching ballad that never failed to bring down the house.

Another important building in the early days was Ott's Assay Office, located on Coyote Street at the end of Commercial. The assay office played a crucial role in the lives of the miners who brought ore samples to be tested here. A bad assay could spell financial ruin, while a good result might make a man's—or many men's—fortune. The most famous claim assayed here came from Virginia City: It was the start of the Comstock Lode in 1859, a strike that produced hundreds of millions of dollars worth of silver and built the city of San Francisco into a metropolis.

Assay Office

Next door to the assay office is the headquarters of the South Yuba Canal, a State Historical Landmark. Built in 1855 with additions coming as late as 1880, the South Yuba Canal system brought water for hydraulic mining in its 275 miles of ditches. At one point, the water passed through a 3,100-foot-long tunnel. The building currently houses the Nevada City Chamber of Commerce and Bicentennial Museum.

Another fascinating and distinctive old building is the National Hotel on Broad Street. The facade covers four separate buildings built during the 1850s. Besides the hotel— the oldest continuously operated hostelry in the state—the building once housed the Western Union Telegraph Office and the Wells Fargo Express Office.

National Hotel

No description of old buildings or the history behind them can adequately convey the charm of the region or the hospitality of its citizens. The Grass Valley/Nevada City area stands high in both categories.

The district between the two towns, Glenbrook, has a history nearly as long as the other two. Although not a gold camp, Glenbrook flourished during the late nineteenth and early twentieth centuries as a bedroom community for its large neighbors.

Glenbrook

Sidetrips in Nevada County

Malakoff Diggins and North Bloomfield: Foremost on
the list of any itineraries should be the North Bloomfield
Road, easily found off Highway 49 on the right as you leave
Nevada City. The road crosses the South Fork of the Yuba
and continues on to Malakoff Diggins State Park. Here a
permanent monument has been established to the miners and
engineers who developed the hydraulic mining process with
its attendant technology—and ecological disaster.

A few of the firsts ascribed to Nevada City have already
been mentioned in the section on Coyoteville, including the
first use of the long tom, hydraulic mining, and the ground
sluice. The long tom is merely an extension of the earlier
rocker box, or cradle, which was introduced by Isaac
Humphries at Coloma only a few weeks after the first
discovery of gold. Humphries learned to use the cradle in his
native Georgia, where the long tom was also invented.

Both the long tom and the cradle, as well as the later sluice
lines, used the same principle for the extraction of gold from
sands with which it was mingled ages ago in stream beds and
prehistoric lakes. The miner's pan was seldom used as
anything besides an assaying tool. A pan-full of gravel could
easily be washed to determine whether a prospect was worth
working. If any "color" was left in the bottom of the pan,
indicating that gold was present, another pan was washed to
determine if there was plenty of gold or if the first pan was
just a fluke.

The cradle was simply a box affixed to two rockers and
provided with a handle so that a man could rock it back and
forth easily. Its construction was rugged and durable, of
hand-hewn wood, since the weight of the gravel it held was
considerable. Lumber from sawmills was, of course, un-
available. The bottom of the box lay at a slight angle to
permit a gradual flow of water from one end to the other.

Cleats, or riffles, were nailed at right angles to the flow of
water on the bottom of the box. The riffles caught the
heavier particles of sand, composed largely of gold and
magnetized iron (which gave gold-bearing sand its black
color), while permitting the larger particles to pass over
them and out of the box.

Cradle-rocking *(Nordhoff's California)*

The riffles imitated nature, for gold was often caught by sand bars protruding out into the main stream of the river. A large proportion of the mining camps were located on such bars, as their names attest: Big Bar, Rich Bar, Negro Bar, and the rest.

One man tended the cradle, dashing ladles of water over the hopper at the higher end of the box, while other men brought sand to be washed. If the sand was difficult to dislodge from the rocks, as many as four men could be occupied in the digging while one man washed.

The long tom was more efficient than the cradle. It was an "inclined, stationary wooden box from ten to thirty feet in length, one and one-half feet in width at the upper end, and widening at the lower end." This trough emptied into a four- or five-foot-long riffle box through a metal plate in the bottom of the trough. One man shoveled in dirt while several others stirred it with shovels or forks to assist the smaller particles in sinking to the bottom. The long tom

long tom

Long Toms and Ripple-Boxes

The apparatus generally used for washing was a "long tom," which was nothing more than a wooden trough from twelve to twenty-four feet long, and about a foot wide. At the lower end it widens considerably, and the floor of it is there a sheet of iron pierced with holes half an inch in diameter, under which is placed a flat box a couple of inches deep. The long tom is set at a slight inclination over the place which is to be worked, and a stream of water is kept running through it by means of a hose, the mouth of which is inserted in a dam built for the purpose high enough up the stream to gain the requisite elevation; and while some of the party shovel the dirt into the tom as fast as they can dig it up, one man stands at the lower end stirring up the dirt as it is washed down, separating the stones and throwing them out, while the earth and small gravel falls with the water through the sieve into the "ripple-box." This box is about five feet long, and is crossed by two partitions. It is also placed at an inclination, so that the water falling into it keeps the dirt loose, allowing the gold and heavy particles to settle to the bottom, while all the lighter stuff washes over the end of the box along with the water. When the day's work is over, the dirt is taken from the "ripple-box" and is "washed out" in a "washpan," a round tin dish, eighteen inches in diameter, with shelving sides three or four inches deep. In washing out a panful of dirt, it has to be placed in water deep enough to cover it over; the dirt is stirred up with the hands, and the gravel thrown out; the pan is then taken in both hands, and by an indescribable series of manoeuvers all the dirt is gradually washed out of it, leaving nothing but the gold and a small quantity of black sand.

J. D. Borthwick, *3 Years in California*, 1857

Lithographic view of a long tom in operation (*Courtesy, The Bancroft Library*)

represented a five-fold or greater increase in efficiency upon the cradle.

Now, however, greater organization and better construction methods were necessary. Dams had to be built, and canvas hoses made, to direct the flow of water onto the gold-bearing gravel. Organizations called companies were formed in which each individual shared the work and the profits.

sluice box

With the advent of the sluice box, more complex forms of financing had to be devised. Not only was it hard to construct a sluice line, which could be hundreds of feet long, but greater amounts of water were also needed. These were brought to the sluice line by means of ditches and high wooden trestles called flumes. One of the largest flumes was built on San Juan Ridge near the Malakoff Diggins. Called the Magenta Aqueduct, it spanned 1,200 feet from hill to hill and was 125 feet high in the middle. The sluice itself was six feet wide. The trestles that supported the sluice were thirty feet wide at the bottom, narrowing to eight feet at the top. It was completed in 1869 by the South Yuba Canal Company.

With the invention of the sluice, manpower was freed from the labor of rocking the cradle or stirring the gravel— that was automatic. It was only a matter of time before the washing of gravel into the sluice was automatic, too. Nozzles got bigger as the size of the stream of water increased. The only limit to the scale of mining was man's ingenuity and nature's abundance.

As usual, the challenge presented by nature was great. The Big Blue Lead, a huge vein of bluish gravel that extended more than twenty miles under San Juan Ridge, was hundreds of feet thick. There was only one drawback: the ore was so poor that it could not be made to pay. The man who could figure out how to make it pay would be fabulously wealthy.

The work of making the Big Blue Lead pay was not accomplished by any one man or in a short time. It was in 1866 that consolidation of claims began with the aim of creating a claim big enough to pay off. The North Bloomfield Gravel Company was formed in 1869 with heavy investments from Bill Ralston and the Bank of California. Capital improvements would require $3,500,000.

The most important aspect of this development was the bedrock tunnel designed by mining engineer Hamilton Smith. The tunnel had to be dug at the level of bedrock in order to tap the richest portion of the lead, and it had to be 8,000 feet long in order to drain into the South Fork of the Yuba. All of this distance was taken up by some kind of sluice.

The drilling itself marked the first time a tunnel had been dug by boring shafts to the level of the tunnel and then working in both directions at the bottom of the shaft. There were seven such shafts drilled, a procedure that required painstaking measurements, but reduced the time of drilling from twelve years to eighteen months.

The size of the sluice boxes was awesome. Each box was six feet wide with thirty-two-inch sides. Larger boxes called undercurrents, twenty to fifty feet wide and up to fifty feet long, were carefully positioned beside the main sluice line to catch smaller particles that fell through iron gratings in the bottom of the sluice boxes. The undercurrents were fitted with iron bars called grizzlies that protected the wooden bottoms from the larger rocks.

In place of one-inch-wide cleats (as rockers had), the sluice boxes had foot-wide wooden blocks alternating with stones only an inch less elevated. There were 1,800 feet of wooden sluices and three undercurrent boxes (where most of the gold was recovered) in the tunnel. The rest of the length was made up of ground sluices, trenches cut into the bedrock in which the natural roughness of the rock acted as riffles.

The Malakoff Tunnel is now buried under the mud that collected at the bottom of the great pit. The tunnel it replaced, much smaller and only a fraction of its length, can be explored with the aid of flashlights and heavy boots. It is located on the left side of the road near the entrance to North Bloomfield.

With the completion of the Malakoff Tunnel, the North Bloomfield Gravel Mining Company began to pay dividends. (This was not soon enough to save the Bank of California from bankruptcy or the mercurial Bill Ralston from disgrace, ruin and suicide.) The pit carved by streams

Malakoff Tunnel

of water directed by giant nozzles—monitors, as they were called—began to grow.

The two men most responsible for innovations at the Malakoff Diggins were Newton Miller, the manager of the mine, and Hamilton Smith. Miller was instrumental in making industrial use of the electric arc lamp for the first time. Hamilton Smith later invented the hurdy-gurdy wheel (1875), a device for turning water pressure into motive power, although he left to others the task of perfecting the invention.

Before it was closed down, the Malakoff pit was 7,000 feet long, 3,000 feet wide, and up to 600 feet deep. It had produced $5,000,000 worth of gold.

It had also produced one of the first environmental suits anywhere in the world. Farmers in the Sacramento Valley along the Yuba River had long suffered the results of hydraulic mining, which dumped tons of rock and dirt into the river. In fact, some areas of the foothills had been destroyed by placer mining techniques as early as the 1860s, when the rivers overflowed their banks and deposited their load of mining debris, called slickens, on the fields below.

In 1873 farmers brought a suit against the Cherokee Mine to recover losses due to debris. The court ruled that the Cherokee was only one of the mines operating in the area and therefore could not be held solely responsible for damages. The angry farmers continued their fight in the legislature and the press. They had a powerful ally in the Southern Pacific Railroad, which favored long-term farming interests over what it felt were short-term gains in the mining industry. The Sacramento *Record-Union*, partially owned by Southern Pacific, attacked the mining interests continuously and helped organize the Anti-Debris Association in the late 1870s.

In 1880 the dikes around Marysville and Sacramento saved the two towns when waters of the Yuba spread over the lower Sacramento Valley. The incident led legislators from farm districts, exasperated by their failure to enact anti-debris laws, to obstruct all state business and bring government to a halt. The result was the Drainage Act of 1880, which financed the construction of levees around the rivers

to protect the farmlands and enable the streams to scour
their own channels.

The following year, however, brought renewed flooding,
and farmers were able to obtain an injunction against mining
operations in the case of *Edwards Woodruff vs. The North
Bloomfield Mining Co. et al.* Judge Alonzo Sawyer, himself long
identified with mining interests, handled the case with great
care, consuming two years in research and argument. Meanwhile, mining operations continued in defiance of the injunction, and farmers formed vigilante groups to protect
their interests.

In June of 1883, the English Dam burst near the head-
waters of the Yuba, six miles above the present Yuba Dam.
Residents in towns along the river were warned by the Ridge
telephone line to evacuate their homes, but many buildings
were swept away by the flood. The incident may have
spurred Sawyer to action, for he handed down his decision in
January, 1884, outlawing any dumping of debris from mines
into rivers.

The Sawyer decision effectively killed hydraulic mining,
though illegal operations continued on a haphazard basis
until winter storms finally destroyed the aging flumes in
1895. The abandonment of the North Bloomfield Mine and
others on San Juan Ridge has left at least $200,000,000 of gold
in the ground, awaiting some acceptable and economical
way to remove it from nature's jealous embrace.

North Bloomfield

Present-day North Bloomfield is a small, well-groomed
town with only a few permanent residents. Buildings are
opened for the public in the summertime, including a fascinating general store and a blacksmith shop. There is a small
museum of mining articles, and demonstrations are given on
a small monitor originally used as a fire hydrant. The park
offers numerous recreational activities, especially hiking
around the huge pit formed by the monitors. The pit is
slowly being reclaimed by the forest and has a lake in the
bottom. Yet even now, a century after hydraulic operations
ceased here, the landscape is unearthly. The exposed gravel
slopes have many different hues, especially after it rains.

The North Bloomfield Mining case was an instructive
one. In it farmers encountered technology that was on the
verge of destroying the land that feeds us. They won, and the

leading industry in California today is still agriculture, but a number of questions arise out of this problem that we should all be concerned with. Primarily, where does progress cease to be beneficial and begin to be destructive? The Sawyer decision assured that California's rich agricultural heritage would remain intact, but what about tomorrow? Will we have time to act, or has technology speeded up so fast that we will have no inkling of disaster until it is upon us? These questions deserve careful consideration as you gaze upon the open wound left in the earth by man's lust for gold.

Humbug City

The town of North Bloomfield occupies the same site as did Humbug City, founded along Humbug Creek by a group of miners, predominantly Frenchmen. The diggins was discovered in 1850, but early prospectors were so disappointed they abandoned the area, giving it the name Humbug in their disgust. Nevertheless, rich claims were eventually found and the town prospered until 1863. The creeks in the area were by then filled with tailings, which the Chinese carefully worked and reworked to extract what less exacting miners had left behind. With the founding of the North Bloomfield Mine, the place prospered under another name. The schoolhouse, built in 1872, is a part of the park, as is the mining office, where gold bars were minted weighing as much as 512 pounds.

Graniteville

The North Bloomfield Graniteville Road continues on past the park to the town of Graniteville. Known as Eureka South in the early days, it prospered as a quartz-mining center during the 1860s. The town was completely rebuilt after a fire in 1878, at which time its name was changed and it gained new importance as a strategic point in the network of ditches and reservoirs that provided water for the mines below.

The Lake City Road leads west from the Malakoff Diggins to North Columbia, Cherokee, and North San Juan. Just before it reaches North Columbia, a road diverges to the right. This is the Tyler Foote Crossing Road, which clings for awhile to the steep walls and then zigzags back and forth down into the canyon of the Middle Yuba River, truly a spectacular and scenic drive. The Yuba's isolation makes it a favorite among modern-day gold miners.

Hydraulic mining (*Courtesy, The Covello Collection*)

North Columbia

North Columbia was an important site during the hydraulic era; its machine shop and blacksmith shop were both moved here in 1878. Cherokee takes its name from a stockade hut built here by Cherokee Indians in 1849. It became important after the completion of the ditch in 1852.

North San Juan

On the other side of Cherokee, Oak Tree Road will take you to North San Juan, another mining town. Gold was discovered here in 1853, though why it should be called North San Juan is a mystery. Some suggest that the hill reminded a soldier-turned-miner of the hill of San Juan de Ulloa in Mexico City. The Middle Yuba Canal brought water to the district from high in the Sierra; altogether, the canal system included 200 miles of ditches and flumes. North San Juan today has a block of old buildings including a store established in the 1850s and an Odd Fellows Hall built in 1860.

North San Juan stands at one end of San Juan Ridge, a fabulously wealthy gold-mining district with paradoxically poor-grade ore. Three large hydraulic-mining concerns developed this ridge during the 1870s, investing an aggregate $5.6 million and constructing 323 miles of ditches to bring water from the high mountains. The amount of gold left in the ridge is unknown, but some estimates ran as high as $400 million when the price of gold was stable at thirty-five dollars an ounce. Incidentally, hydraulic mining itself was never outlawed, only the dumping of tailings into free-flowing streams. During the 1930s some mining was done with the tailings being dumped in specially constructed reservoirs. The current high price of gold may bring about more developments of this kind.

French Corral

Highway 49 will bring you back to Nevada City, or you can take the Valley Road cut-off southwest for French Corral, an old stage station and small mining camp. Later the town became headquarters for the Milton Mining and Water Company. It was here that the first long distance telephone line in the world was set up in 1878. Sixty miles long, the line ran to Milton Reservoir along the San Juan Ridge and was used to coordinate operations of the sluice gates and reservoir spillways along the route. Thirty instruments were included on the line and dispatches were sent like telegrams at a rate of twenty-five cents per word. Other firsts in the mining inudstry here included the first use of electric arc lamps, the Burleigh drill, and the first electric transmission of power. The present-day town has a hotel and a schoolhouse as well as the historic mining office.

Further along the same road you will come to Bridgeport with its covered bridge across the South Yuba River. At 225 feet it is the longest covered bridge in the United States. Covered bridges were built to protect them from wear and also to keep horses from shying at the sight of water.

Bridgeport

Continuing south from Bridgeport and then turning toward Grass Valley on Highway 20 you will pass the Spenceville Road. Spenceville, located in the southwest corner of Nevada County, is unusual since it was a copper-mining center that grew up during the copper excitement of 1865. The mining shaft was abandoned after a cave-in, but the mine continued to be worked as an open pit from 1875 until 1888. The copper was used as a pigment for paint, in which it formed a warm brown color.

Spenceville

Lying between the Spenceville Road and Grass Valley is the small town of Rough and Ready. The town was first settled by a group of miners led by a Captain Townshend. Townshend named the camp after General Zachary Taylor, one of the heroes of the Mexican War, whose nickname was "Old Rough and Ready." The camp was a large one, as the surface placers were rich. A nugget weighing eighteen pounds was found here, an added inducement for others to come and try their luck. Perhaps as many as three thousand were working in the area at one time.

Rough and Ready

Another colonel, E. F. Brundage, had the bizarre notion that the town should secede from the Union and called a meeting to declare the "State of Rough and Ready." Though the colonel had about a hundred followers, the idea was treated by the rest of the miners as a joke and nothing more came of it. The gold deposits around Rough and Ready soon played out, its fickle residents moved on, and a series of disastrous fires began the work of demolition. After the fire of 1859 only twenty-four buildings remained standing. Among those you can still see today are the Odd Fellows Hall, the old hotel (c. 1853), the Fippin blacksmith shop, and the old toll house, which you will see on the left as you leave for Grass Valley, only four and a half miles distant.

Rough and Ready

Rough and Ready Camp, in Nevada County, so interesting by reason of its simple and effective standing committee, or council, affords a valuable though eccentric example of independence. The township contains about a hundred and twenty-seven square miles, and was very prosperous in 1850, when a miner named Brundage conceived the idea of having a permanent and separate organization to be called the "State of Rough and Ready." He called a meeting evidently in dead earnest, and proposed the scheme; urging that none of them had voted for the state constitution, nor helped, through delegates, to make that instrument. About a hundred persons favored the plan, and for some time he continued to agitate its adoption; but the funny and absurd elements of the proposal so appealed to the miner's abundant sense of the ludicrous that the entire scheme disappeared at last, in a fit of irrepressible and Homeric laughter. It became a topic of conversation in every cabin, and beside every long-tom, for miles; but the State of California was good enough for the light-hearted, keen-witted miners.

Charles Howard Shinn, *Mining Camps*, 1885

Highway 20—Washington

Highway 20 from Nevada City provides a scenic route through the high Sierra until it rejoins I-80 at Yuba Pass. The gold rush town of Washington lies at the bottom of the Yuba canyon about three miles north of the road. It was settled by a mining company from Indiana in the fall of 1849, hence it was first known as Indiana Boys Camp. Around three thousand men worked the placers here during 1850 and 1851—though it was almost deserted during the Gold Lake excitement of December, 1850.

The twin gold camps of Alpha and Omega were situated not far from the modern highway. Alpha was best remembered as the birthplace of Emma Nevada, who took her surname out of fondness for the county of her birth. Emma was a world-renowned opera singer who studied in Vienna and debuted as Amina in 1880. She had a charming and effective voice. Her most famous number, with which she inevitably closed her recitals, was "The Last Rose of Summer," a pathetic air that appealed to the Victorian ear's penchant for melancholy.

Alpha and Omega

Part Four:

River of Grapes, River of Feathers

The truly wild rivers of the Sierra were named before the gold rush, by the Spaniards, who visited this area seeking Indians for the missions along the coast. The first expedition of this kind, the Moraga expedition of 1807, had very little success converting natives to Christianity—either the mountain residents were frightened off by the sight of mounted and heavily armed horsemen, or they had heard stories of the treatment of their fellow countrymen in the missions and wanted none of it—but the little band of Spanish soldiers had the opportunity to name most of the rivers of the Sierra. Since they dared not venture high into the mountains, only the largest of the rivers flowing into the Sacramento and San Joaquin were discovered, which explains why posterity has had to make do with all the North, Middle and South forks of the American.

The Spanish names always refer to some external characteristic of the rivers. The Feather River (Rio de las Plumas) was so called because the original explorers found large numbers of feathers floating in the stream. Needless to say, this is not a common occurrence, and doubtless the river would bear some other name if it were discovered today. The Yuba River was called Rio de las Uvas, River of the Grapes, on account of the wild grapes that grow in profusion along its banks. Yuba itself is only a corruption of the original "Uva."

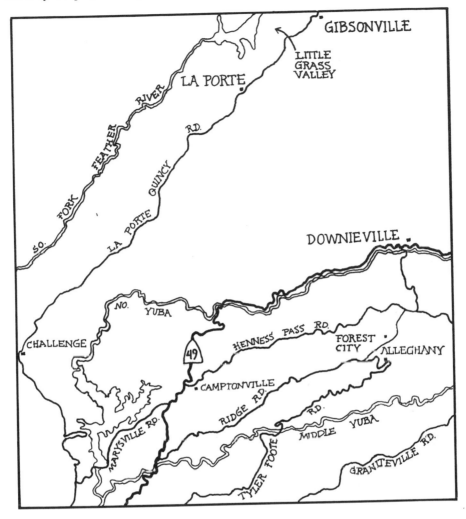

MAP 10.

Under whatever names, these two rivers offer wild and
scenic adventure for whosoever is hardy enough to explore
their upper reaches. The whole region north of San Juan
Ridge abounds in rocky chasms, dense undergrowth (yes,
wild grapes), steep ridges and thick forests of pine and oak.
Unlike the more southern regions, where gold rush towns
stand on bare hillsides, here the towns are likely to hide in
the midst of tall trees, or underneath high, overhanging
bluffs. The region has an untouched, wild air about it, and

the forest has protected the ghost towns from marauding strangers. It is very easy to forget the passage of time where dark pines obscure a horizon of jagged granite peaks.

Highway 49 continues northwest from Nevada City through the forest of the dramatic canyon of the middle Yuba along a stretch of highway reminiscent of the more remote portions of Big Sur. Shortly past the Yuba and North San Juan, a good paved road (Ridge Road) leads eastward along the Pliocene Ridge to the gold-mining town of Alle-

Alleghany   ghany. Alleghany was the last working mining town in the state. Its Original Sixteen-to-One Mine kept operating until the early 1960s, when, unfortunately, a disastrous fire almost destroyed the entire town.

Another road to Alleghany is the Foote Crossing road from North Columbia, near Malakoff Diggins. Originally constructed around the turn of the century as a toll road for the recently invented automobile, the road descends into the canyon along the face of the canyon wall. There are turnouts along the way to permit two vehicles to pass, as well as to allow one to enjoy the magnificent view of the canyon. The last mile on the south side of the river has been considered by some the most scenic mountain road in America and certainly would have to be ranked among the most beautiful drives anywhere.

Footes Crossing is a bridge at the bottom of the gorge where even today gold dredges are active during the summer.

Kanaka Creek   A mile up the river from the crossing is the mouth of Kanaka Creek, discovered in May, 1850, by a group of Hawaiian prospectors—Kanaka was the early name for Hawaiian natives. It turned out to be an extraordinarily rich diggins, with pocket mines that produced well into the 1900s. A chunk of gold and quartz weighing 163 pounds was found along the creek bed; the mint at San Francisco paid $27,000 for it. Some of the mines have been closed only because the pocket or vein was lost due to a cave-in and never relocated. Such is the case of the Red Star Mine, whose owners took $80,000 from a single pocket in 1912.

Forest City   On the other side of Pliocene Ridge from Alleghany lies the site of Forest City, the camp which preceded Alleghany as chief town in the district. Called Yomana, after the Indian

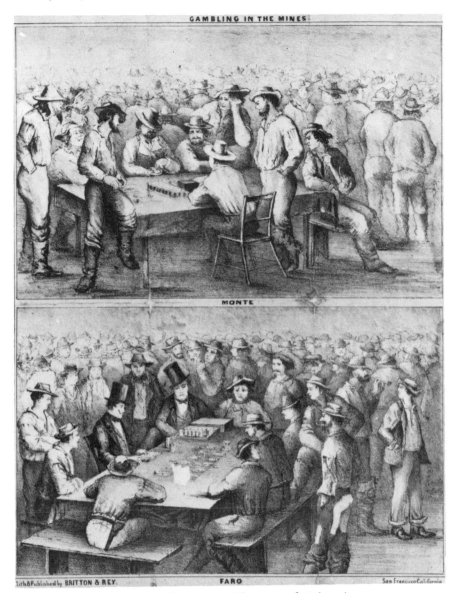

GAMBLING IN THE MINES

MONTE

Lith&Published by BRITTON & REY. FARO San Francisco California

Gambling in the mines *(Courtesy, The Bancroft Library)*

name for the high bluff overhanging the town, or else simply referred to as the Forks of Oregon Creek, it was a lively camp in the early to middle 1850s. Its official name is that of its most distinguished early resident, Captain Mooney's wife, Forest. Like many another of the early newspaper correspondents of the day, Mrs. Mooney signed her letters

Sluicing

The introduction of the sluice, with its various auxiliaries, not only secured the productiveness of California placer mines for many years, but it acted indirectly on society, as a check to the confusion and disorder that began to grow among the miners in 1850 and 1851. Although the early camps were more orderly than those of 1851, they were so, as we shall see, only because the demoralizing influences of a roving and hazardous, irresponsible life had not yet begun to work their full effects. The disorders of 1851 and later years could be checked, and were checked, because they occurred in communities that now had vested interests. As so often happens in social matters, the effects here began to show themselves when the causes were already in decline; and some of the camps of 1851 reaped the whirlwind that the wanderers of 1849 had sown. But sluice-mining meant serious responsibilities of many sorts, and so, in the end, good order. For, in the first place, men now had to work less independently, and more in large companies. And water became a thing that could no longer be taken as it came, but that must be brought in a steady stream to the right place, often by much labor; and thus it acquired a market value, so much per "miner's inch." To supply it in the dry Sierra valleys became a distinct branch of industry. It might be needed to wash gravels found high up on hill-sides; and, in order to get it there, men must build great wooden aqueducts, or "flumes," from far up the mountain streams, so as to let the water run, of its own impulse, to the needed place. The flumes often crossed wide valleys; they were themselves the outcome of months of labor, and employed in time many millions of capital. In various improved shapes they have remained essential to the mining industry ever since.

Josiah Royce, *California*

with a pseudonym, "Forest City," and the name eventually came to be applied to the town.

After paydirt was struck in the Alleghany tunnel on the other side of the ridge, the whole population moved to the new town, which took the name of the first mine there. Though Forest City experienced another boom around 1870, nothing remains of it now. Alleghany, on the other hand, has several frame structures clinging defiantly to the canyon wall. Mines in its neighborhood were very rich. The Original Sixteen-to-One produced $25 million, though it was not opened till 1896. Several drift mines tapped the Big Blue Lead, a deposit of tertiary gold-bearing gravels with a bluish tinge, hence the name. These gravels were deposited when the course of a Sierra stream was blocked by the upward thrust of a mountain ridge. Later, the gravels, which had reached depths of a hundred feet and more, were covered over by volcanic flows so that they had to be reached by tunnels, or drifts.

To the southeast of Alleghany are the sites of Chips Flat, Minnesota Flat, and Plumbago, all within two miles of the town.

The route of the original Camptonville Road might be an interesting one to follow, though it is unpaved. It led from Forest City, north of the present ridge route, past Mountain House and Negro Tent (where a black storekeeper pitched his tent beside the main road to Downieville), to the site of Sleighville House, two miles east of Camptonville, where merchandise had to be transferred to sleighs on its way to Downieville during the winter.

Located on Highway 49, Camptonville has a long history. During its first days no more than a way station, Camptonville boomed after placer diggins were discovered nearby in 1852. Robert Campton was a blacksmith here when the town was named. After the Civil War, with the discovery of the Big Blue Lead, Camptonville boomed again as center of a hydraulic-mining region that shipped half a million dollars of gold each year.

Camptonville

The most famous resident of the town was another blacksmith, Lester A. Pelton, who invented the tangential water-wheel here in 1878. It was about that time that the mines

Lester A. Pelton

around Nevada City and Grass Valley began to run out of cheap lumber to power their steam engines. Everyone knew there had to be a better source of energy, and water power seemed the best solution, chiefly because the 49ers had built so many dams and canals, now no longer needed for the washing of gold. Hamilton Smith had invented a water-wheel that used nozzles to increase the head, or water presure. It was called a hurdy-gurdy, but had one serious drawback—it was inefficient: water sprayed into one buck-et bounced back and impeded the progress of the next bucket.

Pelton and many others set out to solve this problem, knowing that their ability to do so would bring them lucra-tive contracts from the mines. Pelton replaced the wooden wheel, which he found would swell up and loosen the buckets after a while, with a cast-iron wheel to which the buckets were bolted. But he got the idea for his chief innova-tion by watching the way water from a hose bounced off a cow's nose. The angle of the nose, he observed, caused the stream of water to split off to the sides. He therefore equipped his waterwheel with buckets that slanted away from the stream of water and thus solved the problem of ricocheting water.

Pelton's wheel was an instant success, and he soon moved to Grass Valley to get closer to the railroad so he could fill the orders for Pelton Wheels that came from all over the world.

Although the waterwheels at the Empire and North Star mines were used to power compressors, the Pelton Wheel soon found a new use in the production of electricity. In 1879 the city of San Francisco put the first central electric station in the U.S. into operation; in 1899 the Colgate powerhouse in Nevada County became the first hydroelectric facility in the golden hills to deliver electricity to the Bay Area. The electrical industries received added impetus when hydraulic mining was halted and more dams became available for hydroelectric generation. The state of California quickly became a leader in electrical engineering, a position it maintains to this day. All of this due, in part, to the Pelton tangential waterwheel.

Side Trip From Camptonville— La Porte and Little Grass Valley

The Marysville Road leaves Highway 49 not far south of Camptonville and connects with the Oregon Hill Road on the other side of Bullard's Bar Reservoir. Although the river bars along the Yuba and the Feather rivers were among the most prosperous and famous in the state, they were buried under tons of debris before any reservoirs were built in this area. Nevertheless, the road to La Porte and Little Grass Valley (go to the right at Challenge) passes by the sites of many ghost towns.

The remote region on the divide between the Feather and Yuba rivers was first prospected only in 1850. La Porte, then known as Rabbit Creek, was the chief town in the district. It retains the Union Hotel and a Wells Fargo office, among other buildings from the 1850s and shortly thereafter.

La Porte

Little Grass Valley, where Lotta Crabtree lived as a young girl, is gone, but other towns still persist in the neighborhood. At the far north of the divide is the town of Gibsonville, which had its heyday between 1850 and 1870. A few houses remain from the early days. South of Gibsonville, Howland Flat was built on the side of Table Rock. It was a prosperous hydraulic-mining town during the 1860s. Farther down Slate Creek are the twin towns of Queen City and Port Wine—the latter has a well-preserved stone store.

Little Grass Valley

Sierra County—North Yuba River Country

The beautiful green waters of the North Yuba River cascade beside Highway 49 as it winds its way north from Camptonville toward Yuba Pass. Goodyear's Bar, no longer a place of much importance except to the few people who live there, was once a very rich mining camp. Its principal landmark is an old two-story-and-attic hotel.

Goodyear's Bar

The bar was settled in the summer of 1849 by Andrew and Miles Goodyear, among others, and immediately became a crossroads of some importance. The placers were incredibly rich. Two thousand dollars in gold was cleaned up from a

A Visit to Downieville

I had heard so much of Downieville, that on reaching the foot of the mountain I was rather disappointed at first to find it apparently so small a place, but I very soon discovered that there was a great deal compressed into a small compass. There was only one street in the town, which was three or four hundred yards long; indeed, the mountain at whose base it stood was so steep that there was not room for more than one street between it and the river.

This was the depot, however, for the supplies of a very large mining population. All the miners within eight or ten miles depended on Downieville for their provisions, and the street was consequently always a scene of bustle and activity, being crowded with trains of pack-mules and their Mexican drivers.

The houses were nearly all of wood, many of them well-finished two-storey houses, with columns and verandahs in front. The most prominent places in the town were of course the gambling saloons, fitted up in the usual style of showy extravagance, with the exception of the mirrors; for as everything had to be brought seventy or eighty miles over the mountains on the backs of mules, very large mirrors were a luxury hardly attainable; an extra number of smaller ones, however, made up for the deficiency. There were several very good hotels, and two or three French restaurants; the other houses in the town were nearly all stores, the mining population living in tents and cabins, all up and down the river.

J. D. Borthwick, *3 Years in California*, 1857

single wheelbarrow at Kennedy's Bar. Just up the river was the town of Woodville, known to old-timers as Cutthroat Bar on account of an early murder there. Tempers were short and justice swift in the days before any civil authority was established here. One old story tells of a murder committed in a gambling saloon by a Spaniard. No sooner had the murderer done his work than he was set upon by several witnesses who dispatched him forthwith by stabbing him to death.

Not far away is the town of Downieville, the earliest and perhaps the richest goldfield on the North Yuba. Philo Havens told how he discovered Slug Canyon during the fall of 1849. Here the gold nuggets lay on the bedrock of the stream, visible to the naked eye and looking like gold coins—i.e., slugs, hence the name. Havens gathered up as much gold as he could carry on his mule, intending to return the following spring, but returned only to discover the place swarming with miners. Whether that story is true or not, the pickings at Slug Canyon were very rich; it is located on the right as you enter the town. Here a company at Steamboat Bar reported taking out an average of $5,000 a day for several weeks.

Downieville

William Downie came to the area known as "The Forks" in November of 1849 with a motley company of ten blacks, an Indian, an Irish boy, and a Kanaka whose name was given to Jim Crow Canyon three miles upstream. The company reported a yield of $100 to $200 each day during the first winter. According to one story, Downie convinced the townsfolk they should name the town after him by scattering a pan full of nuggets in the streets.

Durgan Flat, where the courthouse now stands, was another rich diggins. There, four men took out $13,000 in eleven days; altogether, they netted $80,000 in the first six months. The extraordinary part of the story, however, is the size of the claim, only sixty feet square!

There were big nuggets, too. At Gold Bluff, two miles above the town, a nugget weighing twenty-five pounds was discovered in the fall of 1850.

By 1851, there were 5,000 men working in the canyons around Downieville, but by 1865, the place had already begun its decline. Nevertheless, a good deal of the atmos-

Portrait of four miners *(Courtesy, The Bancroft Library)*

phere of those early days still hangs around the town, just as
the town's loafers hang around the wooden sidewalks. The
main street appears unchanged, and indeed, these are the
original building that lined the street in the 1850s. But it is
the *second* story of some that you see on the street level
today—the first stores were built too close to the river's
edge and the town was eventually raised to prevent the
annual flooding by snow-fed waters of the Yuba and Downie
rivers.

One of the oldest buildings in town is the one that houses
the small museum. Built here in 1852, the museum has
occupied this spot since the 1930s and has an air of antiquity
itself, one of the old, private displays that are gradually
being replaced by new, government-built buildings. Here,
everything is grouped haphazardly, yet it retains the charm
of a fading photograph—of which there are quite a few.

The bridge across the Yuba below the main street stands
on the site where the most famous of all California lynchings
played out to its tragic conclusion. The circumstances of the
hanging were as follows: A popular miner had been celebrating the Fourth of July, 1851, in the company of his
friends. They had, it is true, been celebrating late into the
night. Before retiring, the Americans amused themselves by

A Miner's Miseries

The miseries of a miner might fill a chapter of woes. Digging and delving with eager anxiety day after day, up to the waist in water, exposed now to the rays of the burning sun, and now to cold, pitiless rains, with liberal potations of whiskey during the day, and mad carousals at night, flush with great buckskin bags of gold-dust, or toiling throughout the long summer without a dollar, indebted to the butcher, baker, and grocer, heart and brain throbbing and bounding with success, or prostrate under accumulated disappointments, it was more than a man with even an iron frame could endure. When disease made him its prey, there was no gentle hand to minister to his wants, no soft voice to whisper words of love and comfort, no woman's heart on which to rest his aching head. Lying on the hard earth, or rolling in feverish agony on the shelf-bed of his cabin, often alone and unattended throughout the livelong day, while the night was made hideous by the shouts and curses of rioters, the dying miner, with thoughts of home, of parents, wife, and sister, and curses on his folly, passed away. That was the last of him in this world, nameless, graveless, never heard from! Meanwhile, and for years after, those he left at the old home despairingly dwell upon his fate. Such cases were sad enough, but there were others still more melancholy. The patient, devoted wife, waiting and watching for the husband's return, toiling early and late for the support of their children, ever faithful, ever having him in her thoughts, and so passing her life away, until hope became charred and black, while the object of all this love, of this devotion, was, maybe, spending his substance with harlots, writhing under the delirium of drunkenness, without at any time bestowing even a thought upon that devoted wife and those abandoned children.

Hubert H. Bancroft, *California Inter Pocula*

knocking down the doors to several of the shanties in the Mexican section of town. Having had their fun, the drunken celebrants staggered off to bed. One, a Scot named Jack Cannon, returned the following morning to a shanty, where, according to the testimony of his friends, he was apologizing and offering to repay the occupant for the damages incurred the previous evening. As he stood in the doorway, talking to the owner, a witness overheard him use the Mexican word for prostitute in reference to the owner's wife. A moment later, the woman herself avenged her honor by plunging a dagger into Cannon's heart.

As noted, Cannon was popular with the rest of the miners, and anti-Mexican feeling was high. Juanita (for so she was called) was immediately dragged before a mob to be tried for murder. While the trial proceeded, Cannon's body reposed in a nearby tent with its wound revealed for all to see. A brave soul volunteered to defend the Mexican woman, but as he gave an impassioned speech on her behalf, the barrel on which he was standing was kicked out beneath him and he was carried on the shoulders of the mob some distance away.

Juanita

The matter of the trial being thus disposed of, there remained only the punishment: death by hanging. Juanita was given a few moments to compose herself (though no priest was available) and then walked to the place of execution, adjusted the noose around her own throat, and died.

Juanita's death caused a stir throughout the United States. It occurred in an era when hanging a woman was unheard of, but the brutality and injustice of the lynching made it even more repugnant to the general public. The miners of Downieville used the murder as an excuse for a general pogrom against Mexicans, and all of them were expelled from the town by violence.

Philo Havens, the miner who discovered Slug Canyon, also pioneered in the Sierra City area, together with Joseph Zumwalt. The two men found many Indians living here in the shadow of massive Sierra Buttes. The ground underneath the Buttes was honeycombed with mining tunnels after the discovery of Sierra Buttes Ledge in 1850. A town quickly grew up around the new mines, but all the buildings were

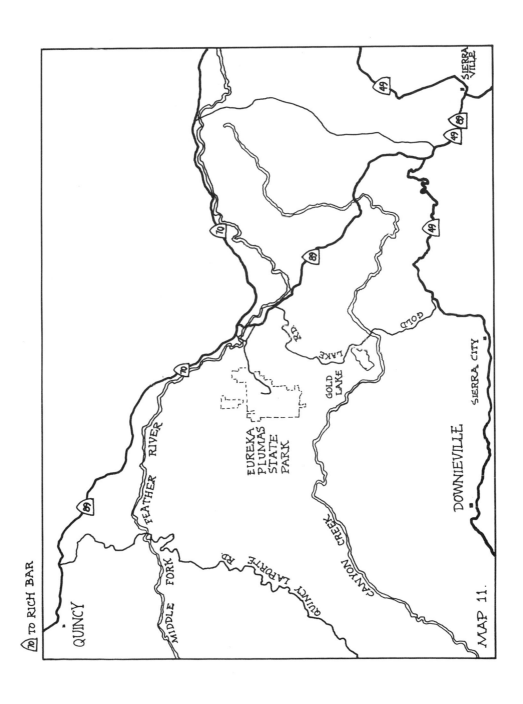

TO RICH BAR

QUINCY

MIDDLE FORK

FEATHER RIVER

QUINCY LAPORTE RD.

CANYON CREEK

EUREKA PLUMAS STATE PARK

GOLD LAKE

GOLD LAKE RD.

DOWNIEVILLE

SIERRA CITY

SIERRAVILLE

MAP 11.

crushed by an avalanche in 1852. The town was not rebuilt in
any substantial way until 1858.

Monumental Mine   The most famous mine in the area was the Monumental, a
small pocket mine which produced $10,000 in a single month
of 1859. The mine owners found no more and closed the mine
in the belief that it was played out. Then, in 1868, the
Monumental was reopened and a single nugget, weighing
ninety-seven pounds, was broken loose from a larger ore
mass. Sold for $25,000, the nugget was turned into $23,000
worth of double eagles—twenty-dollar gold pieces. Altogether, $50,000 was taken out of the pocket in twelve hours;
curiously enough, the mine never yielded a single cent more.

Sierra City   Among California historians, Sierra City is known as the
E. Clampus   birthplace of E. Clampus Vitus, an ancient and honorable
Vitus   order quite unlike the Masons, the Odd Fellows, or any of
the others, of which the order began as a parody. According
to legend, which may have been invented, J. H. Zumwalt,
co-founder of Sierra City, brought the Lodge Ritual into the
office of the *Bowling Green Journal* in Pike County, Missouri.
Sam Hartley claimed the honor of introducing the order in
California, however, in 1857. The name of the organization
is subject to some dispute, but is believed to be "hog-latin"
for "from the handshake comes life." The order's purpose,
though stated by its members as the assistance of widows
and orphans—especially widows—was actually merely the
amusement of the locals at the expense of a greenhorn.

The mark was usually a traveling salesman making his
first sales trip through the region. Upon arriving in town,
the hapless canvasser would head into the first store, where
the storekeeper would make a series of peculiar hand ges-
tures before refusing to order anything. The same process
was repeated at the next store, and the next, until the salesman inquired of one of his tormentors what the devil was
going on. The storekeeper then informed him of the existence of a secret society, the Clampers, to which everyone in
town belonged.

"Fine," replied the drummer. "Where do I join?"

Thereupon, the storekeeper took an initiation fee (which
was based on what he thought the salesman could afford) and
told the man to show up at the Clampers' hall later that

night. Meanwhile, the word was spread to all the miners that there would be entertainment that night and the initiation fee was spent on refreshments, mostly of the liquid variety. Naturally, the initiation, during which the greenhorn was blindfolded, was composed of the most maniacal tortures the miners could think up in their spare moments. It was traditional to hoist the novice to the rafters on pulleys and then to dunk him in ice-water. Something called "The Streets of Dublin" consisted of the man's sitting on a wet sponge in a wheelbarrow, which was then pushed over the rungs of a ladder laid on the ground. The only purpose of the organization at first was to entertain the miners at the initiation of new members, but later the society became well-heeled and actually did acts of charity.

The Busch Building in Sierra City was begun during the Fourth of July celebrations of 1871, when the Clampers were in charge of festivities. Accordingly, it bears the initials "ECV" on its facade.

The original society died out sometime before the turn of the century, but it was revived by historian Carl Wheat in 1931 and now publishes historical works and contributes to the restoration of buildings throughout the Mother Lode.

The area around Sierra Buttes is a popular recreation area today. One of the favorite spots is Sand Pond on the Gold Lakes Road.

The Gold Lakes are only golden in myth. The first stories *Gold Lakes* of a gold lake, where the sands were grains of gold, began to be circulated by Caleb Greenwood, the old mountain man, in the spring of 1849. Greenwood could not resist satisfying the curiosity about the origin of California's gold with a story about a lake he had seen while crossing the Sierra. The story was a tall one indeed: He related how the children had played with nuggets the size of marbles, but that none had been brought along because Greenwood believed that anything so plentiful must have no value. Miners newly arrived in the goldfields urged him to lead them to this fabulous lake, but Caleb refused, saying he was too old to make the trip; instead, he offered his son John as a guide. But the miners who followed John into the mountains found nothing and returned to the Valley convinced they had been swindled.

Gold Rush Mania

Very early there appeared a mania for rushes, as they were called, that is, a hurrying hither and thither after the echoing cry of gold. Whole camps were thus stampeded; at times the wildest stories of new finds being enough to cause men to leave good diggings in the hope of finding better. Almost all of these excitements ended in disaster, like that of the Gold Lake affair, about which one thus writes:

"One day, while in Sacramento city, I heard an old citizen relating his experience in the gold mines of this country. Among other incidents, was that most memorable of California humbugs, the Gold Lake excitement. I shall not attempt to follow the old miner through all his mountain wanderings, nor is it necessary to mention his hopes and fears, his sufferings and toils, and ultimate disappointments— but he made one hair-breadth escape which I shall mention. For many days, the party of which he was a member had wandered about through the snow-covered mountains, searching for they knew not what, and going they knew not where. The party had about fifteen mules, all heavily packed with provisions, and although the snow on the mountains was very deep, yet it was covered with a firm crust, which rarely broke beneath the feet of the animals. One day, however, the crust did break—and such a break! In the twinkling of an eye, seven of the mules were engulfed and swept out of sight by a roaring mountain river, which had been completely arched over by the snow, and entirely unobservable until the crust was broken. Our hero was on the very brink of this frightful chasm, and had barely time to back out and save his bacon. The most singular part of the matter was, that no trace of the seven mules was ever found."

Hubert H. Bancroft, *California Inter Pocula*

That should have ended the Gold Lakes hoax, but it did not. In those days of easy riches and fast fortunes, men believed almost anything, because stranger tales had turned out to be true. In the summer of 1850, a miner named J. R. Stoddard appeared in Nevada City with the wild story that he had found Gold Lake in the Sierra. Thousands believed him and followed him over San Juan Ridge into the valley of the Yuba. At Downieville, more joined the procession of treasure seekers. Stoddard seemed to know where he was going until he had crossed over the ridge at Hog Canyon. Then his memory began to get hazy as he led the excited miners from one lake to another. Eventually the miners realized Stoddard was crazy and went back to the diggins they had so recently abandoned. The whole affair lasted three months and left the new towns of Marysville and Nevada City abandoned until the shame-faced treasure seekers returned.

Today the Gold Lakes area is an easily accessible recreation spot with waterfalls and alpine peaks to attract vacationers.

Not far beyond the Gold Lakes Road, Highway 49 reaches the summit at Yuba Pass and descends into the lovely Sierra Valley. The first man to enter this valley was Jim Beckwourth, a mountain man whose stories were almost as exciting as Caleb Greenwood's—and many of them were apparently true.

Sierra Valley
Jim Beckwourth

Born in Virigina in 1798, Beckwourth was the son of a mulatto woman and a white man. He was large and powerfully built and resembled an American Indian in appearance. He craved adventure as a youth and joined the Ashley-Smith fur-trading expedition of 1823 to find it in the wilderness of the Rocky Mountains. Once in the wilds, Beckwourth tired of white civilization entirely, abandoning it to live among the Crow tribe for six years.

Although there is no independent verification of what Beckwourth says about his life among the Crow, much of it corresponds with other sources on Indian life and customs. He claimed to have been made a sub-chief after having entered a cave and killed a grizzly bear while armed with only a knife. His exploits in the incessant raiding parties of one tribe against another on the plains are recounted in gory detail calculated to chill the average greenhorn to the marrow.

After returning to civilization in 1833, Beckwourth came to California and wound up in the vicinity of Sierra Valley in 1851. Realizing the value of the pass which bears his name, which is the lowest in the Sierra (5,500 feet), Beckwourth first guided a wagon train through it to prove the feasibility of the route. Among the immigrants on this train was a young girl named Ina Coolbrith, later to become a well-known California poetess. The excited child rode part of the way through the pass seated ahead of Beckwourth on his saddle.

After guiding the train through the pass, Beckwourth began collecting money for a toll road through Sierra Valley. During his travels in this connection he encountered *Thomas Bonner*   the redoubtable Thomas D. Bonner, the "squire" of Indian Valley. Bonner was himself quite a character. He managed to get himself elected justice of the peace in 1852 and spent his term of office riding around the countryside looking for cases to try that might help him turn a profit. It was customary for him to settle all disputes in favor of the person with less money, on the assumption that he would have an easier time collecting his fee from the better-heeled of the two litigants. He also required all witnesses to pay their poll tax before they could testify. Whenever his authority was challenged, Bonner retired to Onion Valley, where he held a "higher" court and where he was safe from citizens who had become irritated at his form of "justice."

Bonner and Beckwourth put their heads together in 1856 long enough to write Beckwourth's biography, in which the outrageous lies of the black mountain man were embellished by the sensational pen of the corrupt judge. Beckwourth lived for awhile on a ranch in Sierra Valley before joining the stampede to Colorado in 1859. By no means tired of action, he fought in the Cheyenne War at the age of sixty-six.

Highway 89 leads south from the small ranching community of Sierraville to Interstate 80 near Truckee.

Miners, male and female, in Auburn Ravine, c. 1852 (*California State Library*)

Camp Meetings

The later history of the mining camps affords innumerable examples of the keen pleasure that the average American pioneer takes in public meetings, in resolutions, in committees, chairmen, and "big talks." He does it in sober earnest most of the time, but now and then he does it for the mere fun of the thing. The men of the mining region are even now, after all the changes of the past thirty years, a race of men peculiarly ready to assemble for free discussion, peculiarly apt to have debates in the district schoolhouse, to start arguments, and listen to stump speeches. The early training of miners' courts and of camp life has left its impress upon the people of the mining region. They differ from the people of the valleys as the mountaineers of Tennessee differ from the dwellers in the lowlands. But they have closer and better organization, a more abiding habit of seeking each other's counsel, of meeting in assemblies and of discussing their affairs, than ordinary mountaineers have. The life of the gold-seeker brings men closer together in their camps and districts, and creates links of town life, while the purely pastoral mountains still remain almost a wilderness.

Charles Howard Shinn, *Mining Camps*, 1885

Plumas-Eureka State Park and the Feather River Country

Both the Gold Lakes Road and Highway 89 lead to Plumas-Eureka State Park, the site of a gold mine and company town amid the grandeur of the high Sierra. The park museum relates the history of the mine and has a complete assaying office. The park has never been adequate-

"Prospecting" (*Nordhoff's* California)

ly developed, however, and some structures, like the stamp mill on Gold Mountain, hover on the edge of ruin. There is also a skiing exhibit that pronounces the area a pioneer of winter sports, the first organized ski races in the western hemisphere having been held at Onion Valley in 1861. The various communities in the region competed with each other regularly after that.

The Gold Mountain quartz ledge was first discovered in 1851 and first worked in 1853. After that, gold-mining activity continued until the First World War. Jamison Mine was incorporated by an English company, and Johnsville constructed during the last decade of the nineteenth century. Mine production had reached $1.3 million before 1913, but records are spotty after that date. Much restoration and research need to be done in this park.

Quincy, the county seat of Plumas County, is an old town, laid out when the county was formed in 1854. The Masonic Hall was moved here from Elizabethville the following year.

Quincy

The Great Equalizer

Men pocketed their pride in California in those days. I met in the mines lawyers and physicians, of good standing at home, who were acting as barkeepers, waiters, hostlers, and teamsters. An ex-judge of oyer and terminer was driving an ox-team from Coloma to Sacramento. One man who had been a State senator and secretary of state in one of our western commonwealths was doing a profitable business at manufacturing "cradles," while an ex-governor of one of our southwestern States played the fiddle in a gambling saloon. These things were hardly remarked. Every one went to the Slope with the determination to make money; and if the mines did not afford it, the next inquiry was what pursuit or business would the sooner accomplish the desired end. Thousands who had not the necessary stamina for the vicissitudes of a miner's life, nor yet the means of going into any of the various channels of trade, were for a time compelled to serve in capacities far beneath their deserts, until time and means should justify them in choosing for themselves.

Charles B. Gillespie, *Century Magazine*

Rich Bar

Shirley Letters

The Feather River Highway (70) is scenic and well-maintained. Heading north from Quincy and then turning west, it passes near the site of Rich Bar, where one of the most remarkable of California's early pioneers lived for a short time. Mrs. Louise Amelia Knapp Smith Clappe followed her husband to Rich Bar in 1851. Writing to her sister back in Massachusetts, Mrs. Clappe described the California gold rush in a series of letters. These letters were later published under the pseudonym of Dame Shirley, as Mrs. Clappe has since been known. Her descriptions of mining life have never been equaled:

But what a lovely sight greeted our eyes as we stopped

Riverbed mining *(Courtesy, The Bancroft Library)*

for a few moments at the summit of the hill leading into Rich Bar! Deep in the shadowy nooks of the far-down valley, like wasted jewels dropped from the radiant sky above, lay half a dozen blue-bosomed lagoons, glittering and gleaming and sparkling in the sunlight as though each tiny wavelet were formed of rifted diamonds.

Thus she described her first approach to the mining camp. Her departure, fourteen months later, she describes in the following terms:

I *like* this wild and barbarous life. I leave it with regret. The solemn fir-trees, whose "slender tops *are* close against the sky" here, the watching hills, and the calmly beautiful river, seem to gaze sorrowfully at me as I stand in the moonlighted midnight to bid them farewell.

Dame Shirley's letters served as a model for Bret Harte's later stories of the gold rush, especially his two early tales, *Outcasts of Poker Flat* and *The Luck of Roaring Camp*. It is Dame Shirley's exquisite sensibility that we encounter in these stories, not Bret Harte's, and any discussion about the whereabouts of Poker Flat or Roaring Camp must end at Rich Bar and Indian Bar, the two places where Mrs. Clappe lived during her year in the mines.

The gold rush is more than just a part of our history; it is formed of the legends and the literary visions of those who lived through it. In the same way, the golden hills are more than just a location on the map; the land is imbued with the luster of our imaginations.

Because I feel it is important to read about this beautiful country as well as to visit it, and because I do not wish to compete with Dame Shirley's descriptions of it, I will close with a passage from her last letter, which expresses my own sentiments as well:

> I go from the mountains with a deep heart-sorrow. I took kindly to this existence, which to you seems so sordid and mean. Here, at least, I have been contented.

Index